# Watermarks

### A Teaching Primer for Part- & Full-time College Faculty

*Guiding*

**Don Prickel, Ph.D.**
Educational Consultant
Past President, White Water Institute for Instructional Leadership

**Ruth Stiehl, Ed.D.**
Professor Emeritus, Oregon State University
President, The Learning Organization

THE WHITE WATER INSTITUTE
Astoria, Oregon

EDITOR/PRODUCTION/DESIGN
*RMᶜB Creative Services*

GRAPHICS
*Robin McBride*
*Mary Covington*

ILLUSTRATIONS
*Annette Orrock*

Produced by CreateSpace
Printed and bound in United States of America

For further information visit the White Water Institute web site:
*www.white-waterinstitute.com*

# Table of Contents

*Expectations for college instructors have changed; just being a content expert is not enough. In response to the public's cry for accountability, college accreditation standards require instructors to "guide" students toward real-life outcomes and show learning evidence. The purpose of this book is to paint a robust picture of what it means to become an effective "guide" in the 21ˢᵗ century college classroom—live or virtual.*

There is nothing more powerful than story to convey the complexities of guiding and learning. In this first part, we move far from the classroom into the natural world of a wild river where learning is essential to survival to discover what a good guide really does. Get ready! You are going to get your feet wet.

Ten quality Watermarks emerge from the whitewater story to define sound instructional practice in an outcomes-based college classroom. It's rather like boiling off the sap and being left with the pure syrup. These Watermarks are the essence of "guiding" students toward significant learning outcomes.

## Part Three: Tools for Embedding the Watermarks (the rest of the story) . . . . . . . . . . 79

The Alternative Energy Faculty, featured in the whitewater story, share the tools and templates they created to implement the Watermarks in one of their courses. Templates are provided and may be copied.

## Part Four: Supplemental Materials for Faculty Development Programs . . . . . . . . . . . . . . . . . . . . . . . . . . . . . . . . . . . . . . . . . . . . . . . . 143

## Part Five: Recommended Readings . . . . . . . . . . . . . . . . . . . . . . . . . . . . . . . . . . 155

## About the Authors . . . . . . . . . . . . . . . . . . . . . . . . . . . . . . . . . . . . . . . . . . . . . . . . . . 159

# Acknowledgments

After completing a full series of three books for administrators on learning outcomes and assessment (thanks to Les Lewchuk and Adeline Pasichnyk at *www.outcomesnet.com*), we knew nothing would actually change in college classrooms until we wrote something for the hundreds of new, part-time and adjunct college instructors who are flooding the ranks of college faculty, with little preparation beyond what they saw their own professors do. We also knew it had to be short (well, sorta short) and very different from most texts on college teaching. Without help from the following colleages, friends, and family, this book, specifically for faculty, would not have been written at all.

Our greatest debt goes to the scholars and practitioners on whose research and experience our model of "guiding" rests. Among them are the leaders of the White Water Institute (*www.white-waterinstitute.com*)—"using the river as a 'living' system to advance systems thinking and transcend old educational paradigms." Thank you Marilyn Lane, Larry Lockett, Jane Lister-Reis, Rebecca Kenney, Lynn Null, Dave McKeen, Anne Larson, and Chris Tulloch for leading the cause and inspiring the story. Thanks, as well, to the college teams from across the US and Canada who have joined us at the river. You have validated some of our wildest ideas.

A special thanks to Marie Cini, Vice President, University of Maryland University College for inviting us to work with a college of the future, today. Thanks to the hundreds of more traditional colleges with which we have worked over the years, for helping us see the need and focus the question.

Writing a fictionalized work is not easy for academic types. We are indebted to the real writers and poets who have graciously helped us along: Geraldine Pearson, Irene Hays and Trece Green.

Our gratitude also goes to those directly involved in turning rough copy into a publication. To Annette Orrock for the drawings (what is a story without art?). To Mary Covington for the maps (what is a journey without a map?). To Robin McBride, who was right there when we needed her to put the whole thing together with her special touch.

Finally, we thank Max and Dee for accepting the fact that some of us never retire.

Don Prickel
Ruth Stiehl
Corvallis, Oregon
January 2012

# Preface

*. . . stories are important cognitive events, for they encapsulate, into one compact package, information, knowledge, context, and emotion.*

—Don Norman

It seems that it has taken us a very long time to write this short book—a work that is nothing like what we academics are used to writing. The fault was not in our stars, but in ourselves in that we had to translate layers of educational theory and research into a few pages of story in order for us all to see things in a new way. Like a river, this book is distinguished by its layers of meaning, mystery of story, surface simplicity and deep complexity. We figured early on that there would be no way to do this but through the power of story. We hope we're right.

Don Prickel
Ruth Stiehl
January 2012
Corvallis, Oregon

# Prologue

*T*weed jacket and a pipe? Not any more!

If there is one sure sign that we are living in a period of rapid social change, it is the speed with which stereotypes fade, meaning, instead of a full century, it might take only 20 years. Such is the stereotyped image of a college professor in a rumpled tweed jacket, leather elbow patches, a pipe in his hand, standing before sleeping students in a lecture hall. It would take the fingers of both hands to count the ways in which this image is flatly wrong today as a result of both changing values and scientific research. Still, it scares us that a professor and Nobel prize winner for physics reported that he was totally shocked to find through his own research that *how* one teaches is more important than *who* teaches. (It would be interesting to know if his findings surprised any of his students.)

Here is the real picture. Entering college freshmen in 2012 are far more likely to be taught in classrooms (and on-line) by a faculty diverse in age, race, gender, rank, and degrees of permanency than just ten years ago. And it's not just true for community colleges, which have always employed more adjunct instructors than embedded full-timers. Due to large increases in both enrollment and cost at universities across the board, more and more colleges are turning to part-time and adjunct faculty in large numbers to cover classes. In universities, fewer and fewer instructors are on track for tenure or professorial ranks. It's today's reality. But there is more.

A deeper, more important part of the professor stereotype is the autonomy of the content expert, with little accountability for student learning. This, too, is changing under pressure from the public accreditation commission for colleges and universities and from students who pay increasing costs and face staggering debt for years to come. The real challenge in all of this is how to help all faculty move beyond merely "covering content" to guiding students toward meaningful outcomes. How do we help faculty shed "old school" notions about assessment and evaluation before we put them in the classroom or online? How do we accelerate the speed of change in their "concept" of what it means to teach?

The answer is short—STORY and METAPHOR.

Story and metaphor have proven through the ages to open minds and shift the imagination for both the young and the old. Novelist Ursula K. LeGuin, says, "The story—*Rumplestiltskin* to *War and Peace*—is one of the tools invented by the human mind for the purpose of understanding. There have been great societies that did not use the wheel, but there have been no societies that did not tell stories."

So you will find that this book is like no other in the area of faculty development in its use of story and metaphor, helping us to reflect on social systems from the patterns we see in the natural systems of water.

Part One is all story and metaphor, with deep, embedded significance for what it means to "guide" student learning.

The title, **Watermarks**, emerges in Part Two where the paddlers glean ten (10) hallmarks of sound instructional practice from the story that reframe best practices for 21st century college teaching (guiding).

Part Three is all epilogue, in that it reveals in depth how one program faculty applied each of the ten Watermarks in their face-to-face and virtual classrooms. It's a geological fact that water is the greatest change agent on earth. If our wildest hopes are realized, this story about water will be a significant change agent for a new generation of college faculty.

PART ONE

# Fable: The Perfect In-Service Day

# INTRODUCTION

The story you are about to read is set on the Deschutes River which winds through the hills and valleys of Eastern Oregon where the dry high desert meets the wet Cascade range of majestic mountain peaks.

## Characters

### Roaring River Rafting Company

| | |
|---|---|
| Twyla Livingston | Whitewater guide, age 61. |
| Topher and Jason | Young river guides, ages 26 and 21 |
| Willy Duncan | Bus driver, age 76 |

### Green Valley Community College (GVCC)

| | |
|---|---|
| Greg Gunderson | Narrator, age 52<br>Hydro-electric Engineer, Bonneville Power<br>Adjunct instructor |
| Jennifer Pierce | Professor of Communications, age 40 |
| Bernie Bridges | Chair, Electrical Engineering, age 48 |
| Delco Gossage | Battery cell instructor, age 32 |

### Blake University (BU)

| | |
|---|---|
| Jacqueline Crawford | Coordinator, age 47<br>Joint Alternative Energy Technology<br>Program |
| PJ Plunkett | Professor of Earth Science, age 56 |
| Sonny Chen | Recent PhD graduate, age 27<br>Electrical Engineering |
| Dr. Emma Rae Olmsted | Tenured Professor of Physics, age 48 |

This work, while based on fact, is a work of fiction. Colleges, programs, characters and illustrations are composite representations, drawn from our experiences at the White Water Institute (for Instructional Leadership), Astoria, Oregon.

## Background

In response to the rapidly growing alternative energy industry in the west, Blake University and Grass Valley Community College have joined resources to offer a degree in Alternative Energy Technology. With large numbers of students in the "pipeline," Jacqueline Crawford, coordinator of the program, is eager to maximize student retention beyond the associate degree, into a four year degree. She knows the faculty will have to work as one team focused on common outcomes; but how do you accomplish that in one day of inservice? Jacqueline puts it all on the line and takes an enormous risk, departing from the norm of a lectured in-service to a seemingly irrelevant excursion on the wild and engaging Deschutes River.

 A symbol that identifies a Watermark of sound instructional practice (as defined in Part Two of this book).

The Boathouse

CHAPTER 1

# The Boathouse

*I*'m not sure I am the best one to tell this story. There were eight others in the raft that day—far better tellers than me, I suspect. I'm not really an academic, but rather a hydroelectric engineer who just happens to teach when the college needs me, like so many others. But the story you are about to read so radically changed my old school perception of the role of a college instructor that I must tell it.

Down the full length of Main Street and over the bridge, I came upon the 1890 wooden grain elevator Jacqueline Crawford, our program coordinator and department head, had said I couldn't miss. It stood just above the river with a dignity that accompanies age and defined the "skyline" of the tiny town of Maupin, population 612 (maybe).

Weathered to deep grey by the sun, the 120-year-old elevator was no longer used to store grain from the expansive wheat farms on the dry plateau above the river gorge—the risk of fire in the old timbers was just too great. But as a boathouse for Roaring River Rafting Company and a symbol of old west preservation, it made quite a statement.

I parked my car as the sun rose over the 900-foot cliffs above the Deschutes River and waited for the rest of my colleagues to arrive. All around the boathouse I saw signs that even on this September day, the river would likely be crowded with rafts, kayaks, dory boats, and all those BLM rangers looking for river rats without a license to float.

The first sign of life appeared when a smallish, older lady kicked open the boathouse door. I could tell it didn't open for anyone without at least one swift kick, least of all someone who couldn't have weighed more than 120 pounds.

I first heard about Twyla, said to be the best river guide in the West, after my interview for the adjunct instructor position at Blake U. I wondered at the time why Jacqueline seemed so keen on her. I thought, *What does a river guide have to do with creating a new Alternative Energy Degree Program? At least being with Twyla will be something different. I'm already tired of boring academics. Glad I am not full-time faculty.*

I entered the boathouse and saw Twyla standing next to the scheduling desk behind two flatbed trailers loaded with yellow and blue inflated rafts. She was reviewing her notes from her conversation with Jacqueline and her two younger guides, Topher and Jason. Before I could even say my name, six other faculty burst in, dribbling their morning coffee across the worn wooden floor.

Jason and Topher smiled at the motley looking group—a little older than most of their regular rafters—and hastily pointed to Twyla, as if to say, "This is your group!"

Twyla immediately turned her attention to us. "You sure you guys are up to this?" Twyla asked. Silence. Then, "No!" "Yes." More silence. Obviously, there wasn't a consensus. So Jacqueline spoke for them. "Except for changing our clothes, we're ready as we'll ever be—some more than others!"

I could see from their hesitant expressions that "some more than others" was an understatement.

Together, there were to be seven of us in our raft, plus Twyla and Jacqueline. Jason and Topher's younger set pushed through the door as we hastily exited.

The least ready of our group was PJ Plunkett, a long-term professor at Blake, newly appointed to teach in the Alternative Energy Program. I was surprised that Dr. Plunkett had shown up at all; he was tenured and didn't have to come.

When Jacqueline announced her plans several weeks ago for our in-service day on the river with Twyla, PJ Plunkett had forcefully objected. None of us knew why at the time. Evidently, ten years before, he had experienced a frightening incident on the unpredictable Klickitat River, just north of the Deschutes in Washington State, and swore he'd never put his foot in a river again. I couldn't begin to guess what his response was going to be. He just made everyone a little nervous.

Standing outside the boathouse in the chilly morning breeze, I looked around and thought about who I'd be risking my life with on the river. Sonny Chen, a new, young PhD in electrical engineering at Blake U, was the opposite of PJ in nearly every way. Healthy and strong for his small size, he took the world as his playground and delighted in something so seemingly absurd as a faculty meeting in a raft. I expected he would relish the idea of being flipped out of the boat by any one at just about any time. He was the kind who might also send us all in for a drink. I would be ready.

Bernie Bridges, chair of electrical engineering at the Grass Valley Community College campus, was nearly as excited and confident as Sonny, despite his age. Although Bernie and Sonny were to teach the same courses, they hadn't met before. They had lots to talk about besides running rapids.

I had no clue that morning how the two women, Dr. Emma Rae Olmsted (never "Emma Rae") and Dr. Jennifer Pierce, felt about rafting a wild river. Dr. Olmsted gave me very few clues except by appearance. The way she stood aside in silence caused me to think this wasn't something she would choose to do. With her passion for physics and reseach, I could more easily see her sitting comfortably on the bank collecting data on the rest of us—the observer/critic.

Dr. Jennifer Pierce seemed just the opposite—the passionate communicator. In the first place, she was about half the size of Dr. Olmsted and strong in spirit. I sensed she was ready to take it all on, no matter what the challenge. The more action, the better—even the splash and giggle. It wouldn't be enough for Jennifer to just do it—she wanted to talk about it. Given what I was thinking about this whole group, I wondered if it might be the different communication styles that would throw us all into the river.

I was definitely ready for the river. This was my thing! Along with Delco, I was an industry person, not a real academic. I spent most days at a Bonneville Power dam site on the Columbia River and taught for the college part-time. Delco had spent most of his days in a battery research facility in Michigan before moving out here just a month earlier to take this teaching job. Truth is, running the river isn't our challenge; college teaching is.

Twyla took little time sizing up each of us as we waited patiently in line to use the one honeypot outside the boathouse. I am sure it didn't look like we had much in common beyond just the new degree program in alternative energy technology. We weren't even all from one college—rather, a weird mix of university, community college, and industry folk.

After Twyla had talked with each of us, I heard Jacqueline fill Twyla in on her intentions.

*Envisioning Real-life Outcomes*

"As you can see, we're strong as individuals, but not much of a team yet. After today, I hope to see that we can talk openly with each other, share information freely, trust each other's decisions, rely on each other—the kind of things that don't just automatically happen in a college culture. Even more than that, I am looking for a real shift away from the traditional notion of just teaching content, to guiding students toward common outcomes. I know it's a tall order for one day. But if anyone can do it, I've heard you can."

Twyla responded, "I appreciate the clarity and admire your high expectations. I have an additional expectation. I want every individual to feel comfortable enough with their river skills that by the end of this trip they'd choose to do it again."

Hearing this conversation gave me a glimpse of why we were really here. I just didn't have a clue, yet, how this experience would get us there.

*Mapping the Journey*

When the bathroom was finally empty and Twyla had everyone's attention, she turned to a large map on the side of the boathouse and explained the whole learning experience. "We'll *put in* at Harpham Flats and navigate through increasingly difficult rapids for a *take-out* down here at Sandy Beach six hours later. By then we will all be famished and ready for dinner on the beach. When

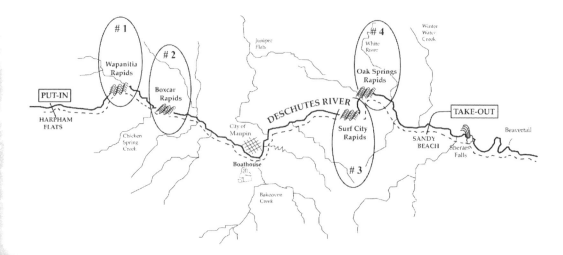

we are sufficiently recovered, we'll bus down here to Beavertail to review the day and watch the stars come out tonight."

She handed us the liability waivers required by the rafting company and their insurance partners. No one hesitated long to sign except PJ Plunkett. Twyla took notice and asked if PJ Plunkett would tell all of us his story.

"It was ten years ago. A full two inches of rain had fallen on our tent the night before we ran the Klickitat with a guide who had been on the river just once before. We lost our guide within the first 15 minutes and found ourselves pinned to a rock in the middle of the river. We were lucky to make it out. I have not been on a river since."

Twyla touched his arm and said, "PJ, this isn't the Klickitat; this river is fully predictable. I know this river and you will be safe in my raft."

*Building Community*

It was obvious to me that Twyla knew the Klickitat. She knew that, unlike the Deschutes, it is highly sensitive to rainfall with rapid fluctuation in water levels. In inclement weather, it is enough to make even the most experienced guide think twice.

Twyla didn't pretend to know everything. Every day on the river she probably learned something new, but she had watched so many good and bad river guides over the years that she seemed pretty certain for herself what made the difference. At the same time, she told us, "It is the paddlers who get the guide down the river, not the other way around."

We stood aside as Topher and Jason swung open wide the barn doors and pulled the rafts onto the trailer. Jumping up high on the trailer, moving like a woman twenty years younger, Twyla strapped in a few extra paddles, attached a bowline to one of the *D-rings* for the *tie-up*, loaded the *throw bag*, counted the life-jackets and zipped-up the *dry bag*. She was ready.

*A river is much more than water flowing between two banks. It creates a corridor of biodiversity, restoring the whole landscape through which it passes.*

—Lanz Claus

Willy, the bus driver

# CHAPTER 2

# The Bus

A cloud of dust in the morning sun announced the arrival of one of the old school buses used as a shuttle for rafters. Tired school buses line the streets of little rafting towns like Maupin. Some still run, others don't. Willy's ran.

To describe Willy's bus was to describe Willy himself. It was hard to separate the two: tall, strong, old, weather-beaten and fiercely dependable. The word *school* had been removed from the sides of the bus long ago, but Willy's veteran ball cap looked like it hadn't been removed since the Korean War.

As I got to know Willy (and it didn't take long), there was nothing offensive about the "girlie" slogan on his hat, which was in perfect keeping with the tattoo of the south Pacific beauty on his arm. It rather surprised me that even Dr. Emma Rae Olmsted appeared to appreciate how the bus's torn seats, worn gears, rusty skin, and sagging springs contributed to the high desert river experience, at least until a few minutes later. None of the others complained at the absence of travel luxuries.

In all, twenty-one people stood in line to take seats on the bus—Twyla's team of eight college instructors and two high school groups of seven each—one group with Jason and the other with Topher.

Dr. Olmsted, the first in line and the first to sit, didn't stay down long. She jumped out of the seat screaming, "My pants are wet!" as water ran off her soggy bottom. It wasn't just her seat. Throughout the bus, exposed sponge under the torn seat coverings had absorbed gallons of water from previous rafters. Delco and I laughed out loud as we took our seats.

Willy closed the door and did his head count, "Eight with Twyla, seven with Jason, seven with Topher, one trailer, three rafts."

After three long grinds and a couple false starts, Willy headed the bus north, downriver, on an access road which had once been tracks for the 1911 Des Chutes Railroad. The ride felt like they forgot to take up the ties.

*Envisioning Real-life Outcomes*

Twenty minutes later we rolled to a stop at a place called Sandy Beach—the take-out. It was part of Twyla's plan to show us the *finish line* before traveling to the put-in at Harpham Flats.

As Willy turned and headed back upriver, we strained our necks to scout every rapid knowing that this was the water we'd be paddling through. Willy glued his eyes to the narrow winding road between the river and the canyon wall, even though everyone seemed to already trust that he could drive it with his eyes closed.

*Mapping the Journey*

In no time at all, Twyla pointed out the right side of the bus toward what would be the final big test of our run. We saw a boulder the size of two buses split the river into two chutes, the right side a difficult Class IV rapid and the left a Class III rapid. This was Oak Springs.

Jennifer spoke what I was just thinking. "I can't believe we're going to get in one of those tubes and float down either chute! Are we ready for this?" Twyla assured her, "By the time we get here, we'll be ready. We'll prove ourselves on the smaller ones before we ever get to Oak Springs." Twyla sized up the different reaction to seeing Oak Springs and reassured PJ Plunkett with the wink of an eye. Dr. Olmsted said nothing while, along with Sonny and Bernie, I yelled "Bring it on, bring it on!"

The day heated up and the air got dustier with each mile. I watched Bernie struggle to close his window to keep the dust out, and as if in retaliation, PJ Plunkett dropped his window with a bang to cool things off. I thought to myself, *The only thing we all seem to have in common is a growing appreciation for the soggy, cool seats.*

*Envisioning Real-life Outcomes*

Just as I was starting to grow tired of the washboard road, Willy pulled off just short of a sudden drop-off at Class III Boxcar Rapid. We watched with apprehension as a raft approached and became completely engulfed in whitewater. Twyla called out, "Watch how they come out of it." And they did! "They came out of it right because they got into it right. You're going to learn to do the same. Don't sweat it." Willy shut off the motor and opened his stash of cold bottled water. It was Willy's teaching moment about the safety of staying hydrated in the high desert.

Above Boxcar, Twyla pointed out several smaller wake-up rapids and a long stretch of flat water that would literally give us our first taste of the Deschutes and prepare us for what would come. Twyla remarked, "It still amazes me how perfect the river is laid out for first time rafters. It progresses from easy to more challenging rapids with appropriate sections of flat water for skill building."

By 9:30 that morning, we had scouted the whole trip, but we hadn't yet experienced a thing.

Creating Energy-
Generating
Challenges

Building
Proficiency

*It is the story, always the story, that precedes and follows the journey.*
*—Terry Tempest Williams*

Put-in at Harpham Flats

CHAPTER 3

# Harpham Flats

As Willy brought the bus to a halt, Sonny, Jennifer, and I were the first to exit and high-step across the boulder-strewn riverbank. The mid-morning sun hit the water and cast away the morning chill. Jennifer commented on the way the river "giggled, laughed and teased the shore"—not exactly the way any of the rest of us would have described it. We were still envisioning those wicked rapids we had just seen.

The last one off the bus, Dr. Olmsted picked her way carefully among the rocks down to the river, wishing she hadn't decided to wear new white Keds. PJ Plunkett rushed toward the bathroom.

A large sign next to the bathroom described Harpham Flats as a "full service" (meaning, no honey-pots) raft-launching park paid for by the fees each of us had ponied up at the boathouse. Had Plunkett known he'd get a real flushing toilet, he might not have earlier complained so loudly about the charge.

All of us, except PJ Plunkett and Dr. Olmsted, helped Jason and Topher get the rafts into the water. Twyla climbed to the back of the empty trailer and called to everyone, "I need your attention. Now! Gregg, you too!" (I seem to always get called out). "I need your attention. Where is PJ?" All eyes turned to the full-service men's room. Sensing it might be a while, Twyla, Jason, and Topher gave us our paddles and fit us into our life jackets.

Once we were all present, Twyla began her *put-in talk*. I knew that the put-in talk is something all guides do to prepare for a safe run on the river, but Twyla did it better than most. Through her demonstrations, she made sure everyone knew the importance of safety and how to respond to unpredictable situations. She checked every *T-grip*, saying, "To your neighbor, your paddle is the most dangerous thing in the raft."

*Analyzing Outcomes for Essential Content*

Twyla didn't assume anything when it came to safety issues. She asked Sonny to help with the *throw bag* demonstration of a water rescue. With Sonny standing a few feet into the water, Twyla threw the bag just over his head with its 70 feet of rope, and role-played an out-of-the-boat water retrieval. While scary to some, the rope was nevertheless our assurance should we find ourselves out of the raft.

Building Community

Twyla turned to us and asked, "Is there something else I need to do for anyone before we make our final preparations?" Dr. Olmsted quickly responded, "I need you to place me in the part of the raft where I won't get wet." Twyla said, "Dr. Olmsted, there probably won't be a dry seat anywhere, but I'll place you right at my side."

The last thing Twyla did was to take a handful of rubber wrist bands from her bag. The wrist bands were one of Twyla's ways of beginning to build a learning community. The bands were of three colors: blue, red and yellow. As a way of determining the different skill levels among the paddlers, she asked us to assess ourselves and take just one band.

Building Community

She said, "Take a blue band if you consider yourself already pretty skilled in getting down this river—you know you can do it. Take red if you have some concerns but not any real fears—you'll make it with some help. Take yellow if it all feels scary."

The bands were a subtle way of expressing to each other our respective degrees of vulnerability before getting on the river. No one hesitated in putting on a band. In our raft we had three blues, two reds and three yellows. Twyla told us, "Mark my word, we will all be blue or red by the time we finish at Sandy Beach."

Building Proficiency

Jason and Topher pushed their rafts out first. Twyla secured our raft at the bank as each of us stepped onto the spongy floor and fought to keep our balance. Some of us looked like children just learning to walk: one step, fall, another step, down again. Sonny and I rushed and nearly fell over the others. Twyla motioned to Jennifer to take the front position across from Bernie, leaving Sonny, Jacqueline, Delco, and me to fill the middle. Plunkett held back momentarily and then followed Dr. Olmsted to the back at Twyla's suggestion. I wondered just how much difference Twyla thought our positions would make.

I watched thoughtfully as Twyla pushed the raft from the bank, boarded the rear, and sat high on the tube. How different this was from what I had expected. My experience had been with oar rafting. I whispered to Sonny, "Until they gave all of us a paddle, I thought Twyla would be oaring us through the rapids. It's OK with me; I'd rather do the work myself anyway."

The raft began to drift slowly down the bank. An undercurrent of excitement stirred within each of us as we began to rock and bounce across the ripples into the river's strong current. Jennifer yelled, "No turning back now."

*The life of the mind is not the rotation of a machine through a cycle of fixed phases, but the flow of a torrent through its mountain-bed, scattering itself in spray as it plunges over a precipice and pausing in the deep transparency of a rockpool.*

—R. G. Collingwood

Wapanitia, the wake-up rapid

# CHAPTER 4
# Wapanitia Rapid

The second we caught the energy of the main current, it dropped us into a long stretch of flat water with intermittent riffles. It was just what we needed to begin to get our act together. Putting nine paddles in the water was one thing; using them to control the raft's movement at a moment's notice was something quite different.

Building Community

Twyla taught us the basic paddling skills and commands. I was surprised that Twyla could use just simple commands to move us through the placid waters:

Analyzing Outcomes for Essential Content

FORWARD PADDLE

LEFT PADDLE

RIGHT PADDLE

BACK PADDLE

DIG.

As we developed skill, we also began to learn a language—a river language with deep conceptual meaning: *command, dig, dig together, riffle, synchronize.* We continued to pick up the language as Twyla taught us to read the river: *tongue, strainer, eddy, confluence, boulder garden, Maytag hole, channel switching, maneuverability,* and *tube-suck* (of which she said, "Only if you're caught in one will you fully understand.").

Knowing the flat water wouldn't last long, we practiced Twyla's commands over and over again until we could move the raft together. I wouldn't have

Building Proficiency

described it as synchronized—yet.

With trepidation we peered straight ahead at the first rapid.

Twyla called it a *riffle-of-a-rapid*, just big enough to give us a bit of confidence. It illustrated the need to follow her commands and synchronize with Bernie, the lead paddler at the front left. Even this tiny rapid taught us a big lesson: teamwork is not an option. At the same time, we were each having a different experience.

The riffle lulled Sonny and Delco into a bit of false confidence. PJ Plunkett sat rather rigid without much expression. Dr. Olmsted kept one eye on the safety rope that circled the raft just above the water line, while Jennifer, Bernie, and I were simply anxious to get into the big stuff.

Twyla guided us into an eddy where we lost the current entirely and had to dig deep to move at all. She wanted us to take notice of the current from afar as another raft passed. Seeing another spongy, overstuffed tube respond to the current was part of our learning to read the river's hydraulics.

*Building Proficiency*

As we paddled back into the current, Twyla said, "You're never safe until you can read the river. A healthy river is never in a steady state. It never really rests. Learning to read changes in the river requires more than knowing the language; it means you have to listen."

At first, only Twyla and I heard the distant sound of Wapanitia Rapid. But I thought it was a distant train on the Oregon Trunk Railway that follows the western bank of the river. PJ asked Twyla how far it was to the first rapid just as it became apparent.

FORWARD PADDLE

DIG

*Creating Energy-Generating Challenges*

KEEP DIGGING

KEEP DIGGING

LINE IT UP . . . LEFT PADDLE

KEEP PADDLING

Faster than I expected, the front of the raft dropped into the hole, pitched high in the air, and torrents of water swamped the back. Up front, Bernie and Jennifer emerged from the hole in a froth of whitewater as a thunderous wave hit Sonny broadside so hard that he struggled to stay in the raft. Delco and PJ were able to keep paddling. I stopped paddling and turned to watch Dr. Olmsted holding on to the rope through the whole rapid, and nearly losing her paddle. Then, as if shot from a cannon, the river spit the raft out of the rapids into flat water.

STOP

RIGHT PADDLE

Following Twyla's commands, we eddied-out behind an outcropping of rock on the right and looked back at Wapanitia. The eddy gave us enough protection for Twyla to help us assess what we had not done so well. Twyla gave us her assessment. "As a team, we could have done worse. There is a reason for every rapid, and the reason for Wapanitia is merely to wake us up to the power of the river and make some necessary corrections." Her corrections were specific. I don't recall what she told the others, but I remember her words to me. "When I say 'dig,' you have to paddle through the entire rapid. Don't cut it short, Greg!"

*Assessing to Assist*

Squeezing the water from her hat, Dr. Olmsted's expression showed a tiny sense of satisfaction. "I know, I grabbed the rope! It was just too damn hard to keep digging when I had nothing to hold me in. I'm still here, am I not?" at which everyone cheered.

To re-enter the current, Twyla directed us to position the raft's stern toward the right shore as we pulled to the center of the river.

*It takes time for a river to find its way to shape the face of this land—drop by drop—then rills, trickles, creeks, brooks and streams. Still, it's a geological fact that water against rock, water always wins.*

*—R. E. Stiehl*

Boxcar Rapid, "not a piece of cake"

CHAPTER 5

# Boxcar Rapid

Getting through Wapanitia heightened the confidence of some, but not all. Sonny, Bernie, and Delco seemed to think the whole day might be, in Delco's words, "just a piece of cake." I tended to agree. PJ, although looking less concerned, said, "You guys are just too cocky. Things can change in an instant." Jennifer, with her abundant enthusiasm for just about anything, just wanted to keep going. Dr. Olmsted said nothing.

Boxcar was next, and PJ was right. It wasn't something to take lightly.

The first time she ran Boxcar, Twyla told us it left a lasting impression on her. Being an early breast cancer survivor, Twyla never thought about her prosthesis until Boxcar threw her friend Maxine, squarely on top of her, splitting her $300 boob. She renamed Boxcar *Boob Buster* and never again underestimated its power.

Long before Boxcar, we passed directly over a *sleeper*. Everyone screeched as a standing wave affixed itself on Jennifer and Bernie at the front. It caught us all off-guard, including Twyla, I think. The river even had its way of getting her attention.

In flat water again, Twyla quizzed us. "What would have happened had Bernie gone into the river on that wave?" Plunkett looked at Twyla, "You'd be the one responsible." Twyla replied, "Think about it, PJ. If Bernie had gone out, he would have been forced downstream and away from the raft; it would be rare for the guide to be close enough to make the rescue. Right? So everyone has to be prepared to make a rescue."

Building
Proficiency

*Building Community*

Twyla took us through a rescue routine that sent a little fear even through me. Twyla assured us, "In my raft, we have never had a paddler in the water for more than 15 seconds. Never!" While it sounded reassuring to some, Dr. Olmsted seemed deeply impressed.

Twyla had other ways of allaying our worry. She called out

LEFT FORWARD PADDLE

RIGHT BACK PADDLE

*Building Community*

Our response was quick, sending us in a circular path and backwards through a tiny rapid. It was our first sense we were becoming a team.

Dr. Olmsted broke a smile, and I probably just rolled my eyes a bit. I am known to do that.

*Building Proficiency*

Twyla told us we had to do four important things to get safely through Boxcar. "We'll need to skirt the pillow just under the water's surface, avoid the strainer (fallen trees jutting out from the river's edge), keep up our speed, and hit the tongue. Hitting the tongue, the V-shaped flow into the rapid, will be critical." My "piece-of-cake" attitude faded.

*Building Proficiency*

As we drew closer and began to hear the rapid, we stretched our necks and saw the first sign of frothing whitewater against black rocks. We all squirmed nervously into position. The raft took on speed. Bernie and Jennifer anchored their feet tightly under the *thwarts*. We followed their lead. All sounds faded to background noise as we listened intently and followed Twyla's commands.

PADDLE FORWARD

LEFT SIDE FORWARD TWO STROKES

RELAX

FORWARD THREE STOKES, REST, STOP

*Assessing to Assist*

I felt a strong bounce and my body sank deeper into the raft. Twyla used her paddle to move us to the left of the pillow. We glared at the pillow just under the surface and recognized immediately how dangerous it could be. Then it all happened so fast. We brushed the side of a boulder on the left and caught sight of a strainer to the right. Twyla called out

BACK PADDLE

STOP

In a matter of seconds we moved past the fallen tree into shallow, choppy water.

We quickly regained speed dipping and turning with the current when a standing wave broadsided Delco and PJ. Twyla's voice was excited and serious as she commanded

*Building Proficiency*

DIG, DIG, DIG!

KEEP DIGGING!

We  hit the second drop, then the third.

The whole raft was swamped. Delco lost his balance and fell back into Dr. Olmsted. When the raft shot upward, PJ flew into the air before falling to the floor. Twyla yelled

*Creating Energy-Generating Challenges*

KEEP DIGGING!

KEEP DIGGING!

DIG!

It was beyond my comprehension how we could continue to paddle suspended in the air. One more big bounce and we were safely through the rapid.

But no! Delco was out of the raft.

It had happened so quickly!

Twyla called to Sonny to grab Delco. Holding his paddle backwards and reaching far out over the side of the raft he was clearly over-extended. PJ jumped up and held Sonny's life jacket. In seconds Delco was back in the raft. No more than 10 seconds in the water! This was evidence that Twyla and the river had taught us well, both technically and interpersonally. We raised our paddles in a salute to our success, and Twyla whispered to herself, "No busted boobs this trip!"

*Assessing to Assist*

*Gathering &
Tracking Learning
Evidence*

One of the things Twyla said she had come to count on over the years was the way the river served up eddies at just the right spots—places where the water runs contrary to the river, providing just what you need to get out of the current and reflect on what has been learned. Twyla guided us into the eddy at Bake Oven Creek just past Boxcar.

*Building
Proficiency*

After giving us some time to reflect, Twyla pointed out the things she wanted us to fix. Among other things, Delco certainly needed to better secure his feet under the thwarts. Above all, we need to continue paying attention to that tongue. Getting into the rapid right in the first place would be key to success and preventing a flip.

*Adjusting
Practices Based
on Evidence*

To everyone's surprise, Twyla asked PJ if he wanted to move to the front right. Contrary to her concern about PJ at the put-in, Twyla thought he was ready for the front, and she needed his physical strength in that position. His paddling skills were surprisingly stronger than Jennifer's. They would be a necessity for getting through Oak Springs. Also he had listened carefully to all of Twyla's commands (perhaps out of fear). He would set the proper pace for the others. She was pleased when PJ didn't hesitate.

*Take thought, when you are speaking of water, that you first account your experiences, and only after your reflections.*

—Leonardo da Vinci

Greg, riding the bull

CHAPTER 6

# Oak Springs Rapid

**W**e had been on the river for just over three hours, but the bus ride seemed days ago. The temperature in the high desert Deschutes River canyon had not yet reached its peak, but it was hot by anyone's standard as we moved toward Surf City Rapid through more flat water.

I hadn't thought there would be much use for paddles in the flatwater, but it was quite to the contrary. You have to paddle just as hard in flatwater as you do in a rapid, or you waste away the day. On most in-service days the faculty wouldn't care, but this one was different.

In Surf City Rapid, I took the challenge from Twyla to sit on the front of the tube and *ride the bull*, while the rest of the team was happy just to weight down the back and lift me high in the air. Risky but fun!

Creating Energy-Generating Challenges

I secured my place and let my feet dangle. Twyla said

### LEAN FORWARD

Which I didn't. At least not enough. I tumbled backward into the raft with everyone laughing. Plunkett told us all, "I'm going to do that someday—not today—but someday."

Building Proficiency

Then, Twyla asked us to repeat the rapid a second time, paddling upstream against the current. Attempting to turn and cross the *fence* back into the current, Bernie misunderstood the command and leaned the wrong way. The centrifugal force sent both Bernie and Sonny into the river, followed by a quick rescue. Twyla told us, "Nothing improves skill more than appropriate

*Assessing
to Assist*

repetition, providing you listen to instructions. In this case one misunderstood command put two in the water."

Each and every experience since the put-in at Harpham Flats was supposed to prepare us to safely challenge the river's power at Oak Springs. Our confidence had certainly grown, but our full ability to work as a team remained to be seen.

*Assessing
to Advance*

Twyla said that if the earth itself hadn't created Oak Springs, she would have stolen some dynamite from the railroad construction crew and created it herself. She knew the importance of having a chance for us to put it all together and show what we could do.

We'd been told that Oaks Springs would not be just another river rapid. No one knew that better than the photographers who hung out at Oak Springs. Sitting under a badly torn awning attached to an old Chevy van, they waited all day with their 300mm lenses to capture the action. Young rafters were quick to drop twenty bucks at a kiosk downstream for a snapshot to post on Facebook.

*Creating
Energy-generating
Challenges*

The safest run through Oak Springs was the upper channel. The photographers hoped, however, the rafters would choose the bottom channel with the large *Maytag* hole. The treachery of the whirlpool prolonged their photo opportunity.

Neither the top nor the bottom channel was enough in itself to rate the rapid a Class IV. It was the rock ledges below the rapid that presented the greatest challenge. The two most prominent ledges stood directly in the middle of the river—*Butt Scraper* and *Diaper Wiper*.

RIGHT PADDLE

STOP

*Adjusting
Practices Based
on Evidence*

Twyla guided us into a small eddy near the spring that feeds the trees along an otherwise brown terrain. First, she asked Sonny and Delco to trade positions in the raft for better weight distribution. Then we took a long look ahead, where we could barely see the start of the rapid. It didn't look so bad to me, but I wouldn't be fooled this time.

Past what we could see, the river dropped so quickly that we had no sense of the rock ledges or anything beyond the tongue. We had to rely on Twyla's knowledge of the river.

Twyla pointed to where the river divided into the two channels. The left required entry along a rock wall. Entry on the right channel required staying high to the left before abruptly turning right into the larger of the two tongues.

She described to us the jagged rock shelves beyond the rapid. She warned that when we thought we had cleared the rapid, we would pass over Butt Scraper and Diaper Wiper. Undiminished by the power of the Deschutes over decades, these two ledges, just under the surface, would require careful, powerful digging. To break the tension of the moment, Jennifer motioned that she wanted a life jacket to strap to her butt. Even Plunkett grinned.

*Building Proficiency*

"Which channel are we going to take?" asked Twyla. "You have the skill to do the more difficult Maytag hole, but you have to choose. We all wanted to try the more difficult. Maybe it was just the adrenaline reaching its peak. Things had certainly changed over those few hours.

*Assessing to Advance*

We moved the raft up the eddy next to the wall, turned it toward the right shore and evenly pulled across the current toward the center of the river.

With each stroke, the sound of Oak Springs grew louder in our ears. Heart rates quickened, mouths grew dry, and stomachs formed knots. Still, we believed we were ready. The photographers focused tightly on us from their perch, trusting their polarized lenses would reduce the glare from the afternoon sun.

*Assessing to Advance*

DIG

KEEP DIGGING

DIG DEEP!

STOP!

Pulled by the tongue, the front of our raft dived over the rock into the raging hole where we were nearly invisible to the camera. As we surfaced, the whirling motion put the raft into a spin.

PADDLE FORWARD

DIG, DIG, DIG!

*Assessing to Advance* Those of us on the right struggled to lean inward to stay in the raft under such strong forces. As we dug deeper, the whirling action spun us downward and out into a chute just above the ledges.

FORWARD PADDLE

FORWARD PADDLE

KEEP DIGGING!

Despite our effort, the river pushed our raft right across Diaper Wiper.

*Assessing to Advance* LEFT SIDE BACK PADDLE!

FORWARD TWO STROKES

DIG

KEEP DIGGING

RIGHT PADDLE

RIGHT PADDLE

We had just turned enough to clear a sharp ledge when Dr. Olmsted hit the water right over Butt Scraper.

She high centered on the rock while the rest of us just kept going.

Click, click, and click.

The photographers were the only ones delighted. Someone was out of the raft at Oak Springs. From their perspective, it didn't get any better than this. Surely, these pictures would sell!

Dr. Olmsted sat alone on a ledge with whitewater on each side. She didn't panic. She stayed where she was. She had no idea the rescue could be difficult.

For the third time that day we were in rescue mode, grateful for the experiences we had gained earlier. Twyla knew Dr. Olmsted was not in a safe place.

Emma Rae (Dr. Olmsted) at Butt Scraper

She would have to trust her life jacket and float off the ledge downstream. But Dr. Olmsted wasn't going anywhere.

It took a couple of minutes for us to eddy out, paddle upstream along the right shore to a spot just below the ledges where we could paddle and stay in place. Dr. Olmsted sat calmly. She didn't move.

*Assessing to Advance*

Twyla yelled above the thunder of the rapid

> FLOAT TO US.
>
> FLOAT TO US.
>
> PUT YOUR LEGS OUT IN FRONT.
>
> PUSH OFF!
>
> FLOAT TO US!

*Assessing to Advance*

All of us motioned for Dr. Olmsted to come. For several minutes she didn't think she could do it.

Then, finally, knowing there was probably no other way, Dr. Olmsted pushed herself into the channel just as Twyla said, "Feet first. Protect yourself from the rocks".

FORWARD PADDLE

DIG

We caught the current seconds after Dr. Olmsted floated off the rock. Sonny and Delco had the throw bag ready but it wasn't necessary. The current placed Dr. Olmsted right beside the raft where Twyla and PJ pulled her in. Minutes on Butt Scraper, but only twelve seconds in the water!

"Water is an agent of distortion and change, forcing a person to see things in new ways . . . the river holds layers of meaning, and so it adds mystery to the landscape, a sense of complexity and risk, a sense that the important facts are hidden from view."

—Kathleen Dean Moore
In *River Walking*

Jackie at Sandy Beach, "outcomes achieved!"

CHAPTER 7

# Sandy Beach

The roar of Oak Springs faded and quickly became only a memory. Twyla was glad there was no place immediately below Oak Springs to take-out. It gave us the time to keep working the paddles as we privately processed what had just happened and how we felt we had risen to the challenge.

I wondered what Emma Rae was thinking as well. I don't know what others saw, but after Oak Springs, I recognized an immediate change in our Dr. Olmsted. Her face glowed with a look of self-satisfaction that was quite amazing. When she told Twyla, "I don't know which is the better story, Boob-Buster or Butt Scraper," we were all amused. For the first time Emma Rae seemed comfortable and happy to be part of this team.

*Building Community*

*Gathering & Tracking Learning Evidence*

What was true of Emma Rae was also true of PJ. Strange how it started out— PJ Plunkett and Dr. Emma Rae Olmsted. Now it's just PJ and Emma Rae. That's evidence something has changed for all of us.

More than anything else, what I really didn't expect was how much we had come to care about each other. I think all of us would have been willing to do just about anything to keep each other safe. As I look back, it could have been otherwise.

*Building Community*

A short distance before Sandy Beach, we spotted Willy and his bus high on a gravel bank. It was almost over; there were mixed feelings. We were tired, hot and thirsty, but also sorry to see it end. But not quite yet.

Twyla noted that we still faced two challenges—getting out of the fast-running current and getting out of the raft. "If we can't get out of the current, we'll all find ourselves in a Class VI rapid, known as Shearer's Falls. It wouldn't be good!"

FORWARD PADDLE

FORWARD PADDLE

*Building Proficiency*

Still in the current, Twyla gave the commands.

FORWARD PADDLE

LEFT BACK PADDLE

*Assessing to Advance*

The raft swung safely around into the eddy and toward shore—a perfect exit.

PJ was out first, holding the raft in place. Jackie tripped over Sonny and they both lay sprawled in the bottom. Getting out wasn't easy for knees that had been scrunched all day. We had gained a lot of skills but walking wasn't one of them.

Willy had already set out the grub boxes of barbeque ribs, beans, corn on the cob, grilled red potatoes and stuffed red bell peppers for Bernie and Jennifer. Never did comfort food taste so good!

*Gathering & Tracking Learning Evidence*

As we ate, Twyla asked us to remove our red, yellow, and blue wrist bands we had chosen at Harpham Flats. She said, "A lot of things have changed in the last few hours for everyone. Take a few minutes and reflect on your experiences and the skills you now have. Choose again a wrist band. Take blue if you consider yourself pretty skilled in getting down this river. Take red if you have some concerns but not any real fears. Take yellow if this all continues to feel scary."

When they were finished, Twyla whispered to Willy, "Not a yellow band in the bunch."

*Find out what makes a whitewater river inspiring and you will know better how to inspire learning.*

—Anonymous

First draft, Watermarks of Sound Instructional Practice

# CHAPTER 8

## Beaver Tail

Ten miles of rough dirt road connected Sandy Beach to Beaver Tail. Clouds of dust engulfed the bus as we traveled in the fading light of the evening. We might have all fallen asleep had it not been for the torture of the seats and Jennifer and Delco's obnoxious campfire songs.

At first glance, Beavertail didn't look like much to me—a bit of sage and a rusted barbed-wire fence. It wasn't until Willy passed out the flashlights and held the wire as we climbed over the fence that we gained some perspective.

To the east, the moon rose over the canyon rim as the western sky turned shades of pink. Five hundred feet below, the river curved around three sides shaping the peninsula into an obvious Beavertail. We sat down in a circle on dry stubble with a full view of the heavens as dark descended. Actually, for the first time, I noticed that dark doesn't descend; it rises from the earth. Interesting!

Twyla explained," To Native Americans, this is sacred ground, and you can see why. I just thought it would be a good place to end the day. You have already proven yourself on the river. You met my expectations both in reading the river and working as an efficient team. I think there is at least a good chance that most of you would even do another run. Am I right?" PJ responded, "Only after a good long night's rest." The group cheered.

*Assessing to Advance*

It was Jackie who wanted a bit more evidence that her outcomes had been met. "I couldn't be more pleased with how we all worked together today, and I am confident it will continue. What I don't know is what we have collectively learned from Twyla about guiding that will improve what we do in our courses. That's the bottom line for me."

*Gathering and Tracking Learning Evidence*

She went on. "Don't worry. We don't have to have all the answers tonight. All I want us to do, while we are still very close to it, is take note of the most obvious. Over the next few months, I hope we will be able to take this experience and come up with what we believe distinguishes our teaching, oops—GUIDING practices."

*Gathering & Tracking Learning Evidence*

The conversation began with Emma Rae. "What struck me was how engaged we were, not only physically, but also intellectually, socially, emotionally, and for me at least, spiritually. I usually like just sitting on the bank observing but tonight I am totally spent! The strange part is, it feels good. We really accomplished something. I am sure students don't feel any of that when they finish my class. I don't even feel it."

As they talked together, Jennifer picked up a stick and started charting the key words in the dirt. Even under the beam of her flashlight, they were hardly visible until Bernie used his water bottle to dampen the dust and create a little mud.

*Gathering & Tracking Learning Evidence*

What stood out for Bernie were the challenges. "No one would want to run this river if it weren't for the rapids. And today the sequence of the rapids was just manageable. They got more difficult the further we went until the big one at Oak Springs. I can do that better in planning my courses—and it won't be just more tests; they will be real tasks."

*Building Proficiency*

Twyla said, "Bernie, the only way we could build proficiency today in both rafting and working together was to start from the simple and work toward the complex tasks. In the end, it's the only way to reach proficiency, which was what I was asked to help you do today."

I thought Twyla was right, but I said, "I think the most fabulous thing you did, Twyla, was to transform eight headstrong people into a highly functional community. Every one of us brought something to this experience. Now that impressed me!"

*Building Community*

Sonny replied, "You know, I just finished my dissertation which had to be my original work—nobody else's. For three years I pretty much worked alone. So to come here and have to trust all of you for my survival was really weird. But I am beginning to think that's the way the real world is, and I need to embed more "community" learning in my online courses. I know it can be done, but I'll need a lot of help from some of you.

"We'll help," said Jennifer. "Communication being my specialty, I am always impressed when I see a sense of community emerge. But I am also aware that a healthy community has something (or many things) that serves to draw them together. In this case, we had a destination. The outcomes were made clear. Willy even took us to see the end of the run before we even put in. This sense of knowing where we were going and scouting the journey ahead of time was brilliant. We had the map in our minds eye throughout the whole day. At any given point, we had a sense of where we were in the whole scope of the journey. What an advantage."

*Envisioning Real-life Outcomes*

*Mapping the Journey*

"Maybe Jennifer will allow me the final couple of words," said PJ. "OK?"

"Shoot!", said Jennifer.

"Part of the reason I got into a life-threatening situation on the Klickitat ten years ago was because our guide was aware of nothing—not the water, not the hazards, not our skill level—nothing. If he had been aware at all, we wouldn't have even been on that river that day."

"Twyla, it seemed to me that from the moment you met us, you were paying attention. You were learning. On the river, your eyes were open to everything we did, which enabled you to give us the specific feedback we needed to improve. It's like you were on a quest to see, gather, and use evidence of what we were doing for some clear end. Like you said, Sonny, I am at a loss for how to do this well in the classroom, let alone in my e-courses. I know I can learn to do it, because I've seen Twyla do it."

*Gathering & Tracking Learning Evidence*

When the evening light faded, we pulled out the flashlights and shined them on Jennifer's summary so none of us would forget. We read them together.

Engaged

Challenges

Proficiency

Community

Destined

Scout

Map

Awareness

Evidence

Fun

"I get the last word," said Delco. "We have forgotten to talk about the fun. It was fun. Maybe all these things help make learning fun. I guess what I learned is that deeply satisfying work is fun. True fun is always more than giggle and splash."

We returned to the bus, leaving our words scratched in the wet dirt under the canopy of stars. "That's my story!" We were flushed with humility, under stars no longer seen by most, as they are often erased by urban life.

*If there is magic on the planet, it is contained in water.*

—Loren Eiseley

Twyla, exemplary guide

# Back at the Boathouse

The late night conversation had been much richer than Jennifer's few words had captured. In fact, it was certainly on Twyla's mind when she returned to the boathouse the next morning.

She reflected on the photographer's pictures from Oak Springs that she held in her hands. They were evidence of what the instructors could do with what they had learned about working as a team and keeping themselves safe on the river. The list of words from Beaver Tail that remained imprinted in her mind was further evidence that they actually learned a great deal about guiding and learning. She was pleased with the results.

*Gathering and Tracking Learning Evidence*

Twyla tried to reconstruct for herself something specific PJ said to her in the parking lot just before leaving when she asked if she had met his expectations.

What he said was, "The experience you gave us today was the most perfect in-service I could ever imagaine. Using the river was brilliant. There is only one thing I think would have improved it; we needed more eddy-outs. It takes time to absorb all that is happening. For ten long years, I have been reflecting on what our guide on the Klickitat did so wrong. I suspect I'll be reflecting for a good long time on what you did right. Reflection is powerful, you know. Throw in some more eddies the next time you do this."

Twyla thought to herself, "PJ was right. What we were learning was far beyond the techniques of paddling. This team was there for the deeper stuff—creating a mental model of guiding and taking time for reflection on and off the river are keys to achieving the outcomes. We can find a way to do that."

*Adjusting Practices Based on Evidence*

*If you wanted to create an education environment that was directly opposed to what the brain was good at doing, you probably would design something like a classroom. If you wanted to create a business environment that was directly opposed to what the brain is good at doing, you probably would design something like a cubicle. And if you wanted to change things, you might have to tear both of them down and start—with story.*

—John Medina

# PART TWO

# Ten Watermarks of Sound Instructional Practice

# Ten Watermarks

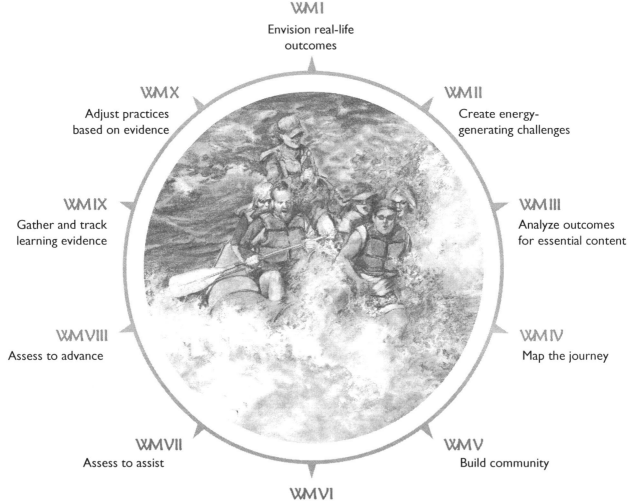

**WM I**
Envision real-life outcomes

**WM X**
Adjust practices based on evidence

**WM II**
Create energy-generating challenges

**WM IX**
Gather and track learning evidence

**WM III**
Analyze outcomes for essential content

**WM VIII**
Assess to advance

**WM IV**
Map the journey

**WM VII**
Assess to assist

**WM V**
Build community

**WM VI**
Engage with learners to build proficiency

## of Sound Instructional Practice

*G*reg's story about Twyla's guiding of a group of college faculty on a whitewater river serves as a metaphor for guiding students in college classrooms. Closely examining what she did on the river provides a vehicle for discussing the changing expectations for college instructors, whether they be full-time, tenured faculty or part of the rapidly increasing ranks of adjunct instructors. Sound instructional practices are about improving learning without regard for our organizational system of rank or seniority.

## Introduction to the Watermarks

*WATERMARK n. A design (marking) impressed on paper visible only when held to the light; often an indicator of quality or authenticity; v. to impress with a watermark.*

The grocery clerk holds your fifty dollar bill to the light to detect its watermark, a symbol, impressed by the rollers that shaped the paper, as a sign of quality and authenticity. In the same way, when we hold "to the light" Twyla's performance as an instructional guide, we find Ten Watermarks of Sound Instructional Practice that are key to student learning in every virtual and face-to-face college classroom.

You saw these quality Watermarks appearing throughout the story with the symbol WM and noted in the sidebar.

| | |
|---|---|
| WM I | Envision real-life outcomes |
| WM II | Create energy-generating challenges |
| WM III | Analyze outcomes for essential content |
| WM IV | Map the journey |
| WM V | Build community |
| WM VI | Engage with learners to build proficiency |
| WM VII | Assess to assist |
| WM VIII | Assess to advance |
| WM IX | Gather and track learning evidence |
| WM X | Adjust practices based on evidence |

While these ten Watermarks continue to validate the vast amount of empirical research on learning over the past fifty years, they reflect a major role shift for college instructors of the 21st century. They indicate the growing demand for increased accountability through a focus on learning outcomes, authentic assessment, tracking of learning evidence and use of evidence to change teaching practices.

The Watermarks of sound instructional practice in this century move us beyond the academy to real-life roles—outside the classroom. They shift us from emphasizing simply what students KNOW, to what students can actually DO with what they know in real-life contexts. The requirement for learning outcomes is firmly embedded in the most current accreditation standards for all colleges across the U.S and in most provincial guidelines across Canada.

The changing role of the college instructor is redefined in these Watermarks and modeled by Twyla in the story. So is the relationship between the instructor and the student (river guide and paddlers), and between the student and other students. Most significant, the Watermarks replace the concepts of teaching with the concepts of guiding. Teaching doesn't necessarily imply that you are on the move—going someplace. Guiding does.

It isn't an accident that five out of the ten (fully half) of the Watermarks of sound instructional practice relate to assessment. Taken as a whole, these Watermarks require a major shift away from the traditional use of rote memory as sole indicator of learning, to engaging in real-life applications of knowledge as indicators of intended outcomes. This shift was revealed in the story, as told by Greg.

While we show these ten Watermarks in a linear, numerical order (like we do with most things), in reality, they aren't locked into any order. When the river flows, lots of things bubble up. For example, Twyla focused on the intended outcomes at the

beginning of the run but returned to them time and again throughout the journey. Twyla focused intently on building teamwork at Harpham Flats and kept returning to it through the conversation at Beavertail. When you look back at the story, you will find no prescribed order. The order emerged with the experience.

The purpose of the following is to bring some clarity to each of the ten Watermarks as they applied not only to Greg's story of the river experience, but more importantly as they apply to your own real or virtual classroom. To do this, we include examples of a specific course, *AEP 212: Alternative Energy Systems*, that the rafting team designed and delivered six months following their in-service river experience. These examples show how the Watermarks shifted the instructor's role from teaching to guiding.

# WATERMARK I
## Envision Real Life Outcomes

At no time in the history of higher education has there been a greater need to be both intentional and relevant to the emerging needs of our increasingly global society. Whether we teach technical, professional, scientific, or liberal arts college courses, it is essential that we first envision the potential real-life roles for which college courses will help students prepare, i.e. global citizen, family member, worker, community member, life-long learner, steward of the environment. Envisioning these roles lays the groundwork for developing clear, robust, and relevant learning outcomes.

While at the Boathouse, Twyla did something very significant, beyond the preparation of the equipment, that gave her direction for everything that followed. She envisioned the participants' role as paddlers. Jacqueline envisioned their roles as college instructors. Both Twyla and Jacqueline clarified the intended outcomes of the trip. Do you recall what they were?

> ". . . to work more fully as a team, (talk openly with each other, share information freely, trust each other's decisions, rely on each other) and engage fully in what they are doing with each other and our students." *(Worker role—with implications for all other roles)*

> ". . . to shift from teaching content to guiding students. *(Instructor role)*

> ". . . to feel comfortable enough with their river skills that they'd choose to do it again, with the technical skills to keep themselves safe." *(Paddler role)*

Here are the three most important things about how these outcome statements are constructed:

*They are not objectives or goals.* Outcome statements differ greatly from learning objectives and goals in that they say what you hope to see "outside"—beyond—after the run is over. This might seem like a slight difference, but it is major!

There is magic in "outside thinking." It helps both faculty and students increase the relevance of what they do in classrooms. Never make the mistake of equating objectives and goals (things you can do in here) with real outcomes.

*Outcome statements describe a vision* of what students will be able to do as a result of their learning. Robust statements paint a clear, concise, practical picture.

*Outcome statements are the guide's "guide,"* and the best ones come out of a consensus of advisors inside and outside the college.

On page 56, examine carefully the intended learning outcomes (Figure 2.1) that were developed by the faculty in the course, *AEP 212, Alternative Energy Systems.* Notice

**Intended Learning Outcomes**

AEP 212 Alternative Energy Systems

*(After this course students should be able to)*

1. Investigate the technical, economical and environmental potential (and progress) of new and emerging forms of power generation.

2. Use the principles of science (basic electricity, mechanics, chemistry, mathematics and computer technology) to fabricate and test energy prototypes.

3. Follow industry quality and safety procedures for personal gear, equipment and tools.

Figure 2.1

their alignment with the above three principles.

We describe the process for developing learning outcomes in *Part Three, "Cogging" Tools*, under the section titled *Cogging Outcomes*, pages 83–88. In addition, you will find a second tool, in this same section, that the AEP Faculty used to help to assess the quality of their course outcomes.

# WATERMARK II
## Create Energy-Generating Challenges

Many rivers offer nothing more than flat water and draw few paddlers. There is a reason why rafters are drawn to a whitewater experience. It churns with energy. It's challenging. It's hard. It expects a lot from paddlers and delivers even more. What do you expect the success rate would have been for reaching the take-out if the paddlers had faced nothing but flatwater? They'd be bored and probably would not finish the run. Does this sound a little like a drop-out or low completion issue? The creation of relevant challenges is one of the most important keys to effective college guiding and deserves to be one of our ten Watermarks.

In our river metaphor, the rapids represent the kinds of intellectual challenges that keep students actively engaged and energized in college courses. In the academy of higher education, we have traditionally come to think of them as tests. But real-life outcomes are often better assessed by challenging students with meaningful tasks that resemble real-world application, rather than solely testing for knowledge. On the river, the role-related challenges were the rapids—increasingly challenging from Class I through a Class IV. In the classroom, possible role-related assessment tasks might include:

- Projects • Proposals • Problem Solutions • Presentations • Simulated Reports • White Papers • Demonstrations • Role-Plays • Portfolios • Debates • Blogs • Research

Role-related challenges go a long way in generating student energy and often serve as a means of organizing how the course flows, in the same way that exams have served in the past.

Here are our six keys to creating energy-generating challenges:

Course challenges (rapids) should consist of the following five essentials.

1. **Plan and create all the challenges prior to the beginning** of the course so they provide destination points when mapping and disclosing the students' journey.

2. **Schedule one very early** to engage students; create a sense of urgency, and assess entry knowledge and skills.

3. **Align challenges with the intended outcomes;** as a whole, they should equal the outcomes.

4. **Make them achievable**—not too easy, not too hard. Every challenge (rapid) should present some kind of risk.

5. **Escalate the level of difficulty** over the duration of the course.

6. **Treat the challenges as more than an assignment;** don't underestimate their power to stimulate, engage and motivate learning.

The section of the river Twyla chose to run with the novice paddlers was critical to

## Energy-Generating Challenges

### AEP 212 Alternative Energy Systems

*What students will do to demonstrate evidence of intended outcomes:*

1. Choose an alternative energy system. Write a position paper and speak to the class for 15 minutes on both the pros and cons of that system from an economics and environmental perspective. (End of third week).

2. As a laboratory team, design and build three simple energy systems: 1) fuel cell, 2) wind, 3) solar. (Weeks 6, 9, 13 respectively)

3. Conduct an energy site assessment and propose an alternative energy solution that includes current system identification, benefits of proposed system and design/implementation steps for transfer. (Week 16)

Figure 2.2

their success. She put in at Harpham Flats above Wapanitia, the least difficult rapid, while the rest of the run consisted of progressively more difficult rapids. This is the same thing the river team did in creating the key assessment tasks for AEP 212, as shown in Figure 2.2.

The final challenge in a course is often referred to as the "capstone," in which the students must synthesize all they have learned. To generate energy, a capstone must be a deeper learning experience rather than simply a final exam. On the river, do you recall which rapid was the capstone? Oak Springs, of course! In the above list of key assessments for AEP 212, which appears to be the capstone? Yes, you are correct, the energy site assessment!

We describe the process for developing key energy-generating challenges in *Part Three, "Cogging" Tools*, under the section titled *Cogging Assessment Tasks*, pages 89–90, which is the second part of a *Course Outcomes Guide* (The "Cogging" Tool).

 # WATERMARK III
## Analyze Outcomes for Essential Content

No matter what kind of course we are assigned to teach, it is almost a given that there will be too much to learn and too little time to learn it. When we approach the content as topics we want to cover, or topics contained in the textbook, there seems no end to what should be learned. When we identify intended outcomes first, we can more strategically identify the content that is essential in a given course.

In an outcomes approach to learning, the textbook isn't the guide; we are! A textbook should be no more than a primary resource contributing to students achieving the intended outcomes. This view of content represents a departure from traditional college curriculum design, in that it defines content with regard to its importance to an intended outcome.

If we don't describe the course content by topics, then how do we describe it? We describe the content by what students must learn: concepts, issues, and skills.

**Concepts** define what learners will need to understand

**Issues** capture the real-life problems or dilemmas pertinent to the intended outcome, and

**Skills** define the learners' abilities necessary to demonstrate the intended outcomes.

With her vast experience guiding teams, Twyla knew exactly what concepts, issues and skills they had to learn to achieve that first outcome:

"...to work more fully as a team, (talking openly with each other, sharing information freely, trusting each other's decisions, relying on each other, and engaging fully with each other and their students)."

Twyla was clear on the major concepts, skills, and issues paddlers needed to learn to achieve the teamwork outcome. Here they are:

| Concepts to Understand | Issues to Face | Skills to Master |
| --- | --- | --- |
| Individual Responsibility | Lack of Trust | Listening |
| Individual Contribution | Need to Control | Following |
| Trust | Poor Communication | Leading |
| Adaptability | Inflexibility | |
| Interdependence | Irresponsibility | |
| | Honesty | |

Figure 2.3

It is easy to reflect on how this worked for Twyla. Twyla only had six hours on the river. It would have been nice for her to have had the time to talk about the history of each rapid—how Boxcar really got its name from a train wreck. With all her knowledge of the area, she could have gone into the geological formations of the basalt cliffs and the reasons the Deschutes is regarded as a peculiar river the world over. But, no! Twyla focused the time on what the students needed to KNOW and be able to DO once they left the river, without denying the giggles and splashes that added pleasure to the adventure.

While the content leading to the teamwork outcome is fairly evenly distributed across the three categories of concepts, issues, and skills, not all content outlines are. An issues course might be all issues. A skills course would show mostly skill sets. An introductory course will usually be mostly conceptual. And some courses are a combination of all three together.

Thinking about the course content in the above way also led Twyla to appropriate learning activities:

**Understanding Concepts:** modeling, discussing, discovering, reflecting, sharing

**Facing the Issues:** problem-solving, critically thinking

**Mastering Skills:** demonstrating, practicing, giving feedback

There is one important thing that makes this manner of describing content so important in today's world. It makes a clear distinction between a surface-level understanding of a concept and the deep learning that is required to resolve real-life issues. Both deeper learning and skill mastery have increased importance in a curriculum that expects real-life results.

We include on page 61, a simplified example (Figure 2.4) of how the AEP 212 faculty adopted this method of describing essential content for their course, based on the course's learning outcomes discussed under Watermark I.

| AEP 212 Alternative Energy Systems | | |
|---|---|---|
| **Concepts to Understand** | **Issues to Face** | **Skills to Master** |
| 1. renewable energy sources <br>   a) solar <br>   b) wind <br>   c) fuel cells <br> 2. fossil fuels <br> 3. heat transfer <br> 4. chemical reaction <br> 5. power systems <br> 6. energy consumption <br> 7. photovoltaic systems <br> 8. hydro-electricity <br> 9. thermodynamics <br> 10. hydrogen systems <br> 11. energy quantification <br> 12. electrolysis <br> 13. PEM (protein exchange membrane) <br> 14. convection current <br> 15. kinetic energy <br> 16. evaluation models <br> 17. site assessments | 1. Safety <br>   –Self <br>   –Community <br>   –Environment <br> 2. Feasibility <br>   –technical <br>   –economic <br>   –environmental <br> 3. Return on investment | 1. Arguing pros and cons of alternative energy over fossil fuel systems <br> 2. Classifying key alternative energy resources according to use, availability, and environmental impact <br> 3. Analyzing existing and proposed alternative energy systems related to efficiency, economies, and environment (high-level skill) <br> 4. Fabricating and testing prototypes <br> 5. Using principles of science to design/test systems <br> 6. Conducting laboratory experiments <br> 7. Working safely and using protection gear <br> 8. Contributing responsibly to the efforts of a team <br> 9. Evaluating energy systems <br> 10. Designing feasible solutions to energy problems. |

Figure 2.4

We describe the process for analyzing outcomes to determine the essential content of a course in *Part Three, "Cogging" Tools*, under the section titled *Cogging Essential Content*, pages 91–94. When the products in these three previous sections merge together, the result is a one-page *Course Outcomes Guide (COG)*, as illustrated in Part Three, Figure 3.3, page 93.

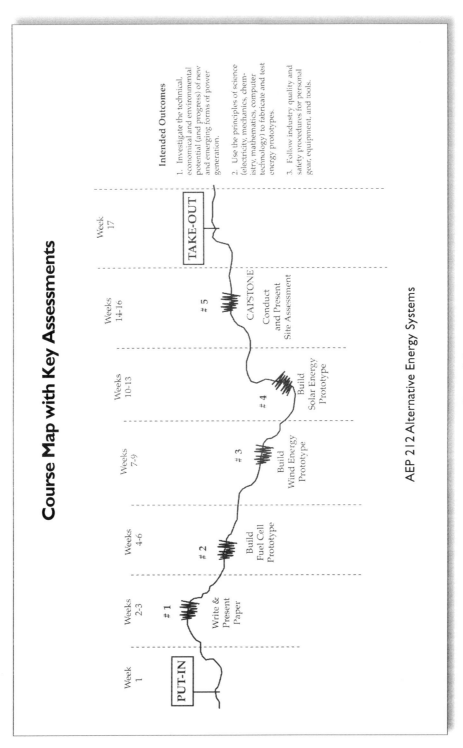

Figure 2.5

# WATERMARK IV
## Map the Journey

**THE BOATHOUSE** When the bathroom was finally empty and Twyla had their attention, she turned to the large map on the outside wall of the boathouse and explained the whole learning experience. *We'll put in at Harpham Flats and navigate through increasingly difficult rapids for a take-out down here at Sandy Beach six hours later.*

Any kind of map is a powerful tool when we are intent on going somewhere. Twyla made sure the paddlers were well versed in the "big picture" of where they were going and how it all connected, before they ever put in at Harpham Flats. For the visual learner (and most of us are visual learners), the map puts everything in context of the whole day's experience—the boathouse, the put-in, the river, the rapids, the take-out, and even Beavertail.

Twyla's river map was created to highlight the major events in the run—in this case, the rapids. It happened that the major events on the river became the key assessment points. So, when it comes to creating a course map, key assessment points are the logical first organizers.

This is illustrated in this simple draft of a map of the Alternative Energy course, which was the first one the AEP faculty created (Figure 2.5, facing page).

Organizing the course around these major assessment points enabled the AEP faculty to accomplish four things:

1. Caused them to think through assessment in some detail before the class took shape.

2. Divided the journey into manageable parts.

3. Ignited and sustained "paddler" engagement.

4. Increased opportunity to assess to assist learning, providing greater peer and instructor feedback throughout the course.

In addition, the Alternative Energy faculty then "zoomed-in" to begin linking the course content for AEP 212 to the first two major assessments in the table on page 64 (Figure 2.6). Notice how the course map as a schedule of activities (in the form of a table) is structured around the essential content and assessment tasks of this course.

This approach to mapping a course assures that assessment points align with the intended outcomes, and that the content aligns closely with the assessment points. This is a very different process of course development than that of covering topics or following a table of contents in a textbook. The purpose of both maps is to assure that the student sees the journey ahead and recognizes that everything is connected to support their success.

We include two examples of how the faculty mapped the students' journey in AEP 212 and describe the process for developing mapping in *Part Three, Course Mapping Tools*, pages 96–100.

| Course Map | | |
|---|---|---|
| **AEP 212: Alternative Energy Systems** | | |
| | **Week 1–3** | **Week 4–6** |
| Develop a deep understanding of these major concepts: | –Renewable energy<br>–Solar energy<br>–Wind energy<br>–Fuel cells<br>–Economic return<br>–Technical feasibility<br>–Environmental impact<br>–Fossil fuel systems | –Heat transfer<br>–Chemical reaction<br>–Power conditioning<br>–Distributed generation<br>–Voltaic batteries<br>–Heating generation and transfer<br>–Hydro electric power<br>–Fuel history |
| Face these issues: | Feasibility: technical, economic, and environmental | Safety: self, community, and environment |
| Master these skills: | How to:<br>–develop sound arguments for the pros and cons of energy systems<br>–write a good position paper<br>–use statistics to support position on energy systems<br>–contribute equally to work team | How to:<br>–classify energy resources<br>–analyze energy systems<br>–conduct lab experiments<br>–assure safety<br>–contribute to work of the team |
| **Show Learning Proficiency (Key Assessments):** | **Submit position paper (energy system) and make 15-minute presentation (wk. 3)** | **Build prototype of fuel cell (wk. 6)** |

Figure 2.6

 # WATERMARK V
## Build Community

One way of defining *community* is a group of people who know who they are, whom they are with, and where they are going. This is a particularly powerful definition when it comes to talking about learning communities. In a learning community, we need to feel we are respected, supported in our differences, and free to make mistakes. Experience confirms that adults seek out instructors who support their efforts and have no hidden agendas; we all want to feel we are safe.

From the Boathouse to Beavertail, Twyla had the ideal circumstances to build a learning community, even though safety was a constant issue and she had but a few hours with the paddlers. In everything she did, she was mindful of relationships. To her advantage, she was physically in the raft and had a small group in close proximity. All these things seemingly made it easy to build relationships that enhanced learning. What made building a community difficult for Twyla were the ever-present issues of fear and safety. While listening to PJ Plunkett's fears, she touched his arm and said, "PJ, this isn't the Klickatat. I know this river and you will be safe in my raft."

While community building seemed a natural result of the intense, shared experience on the river, it has to be more intentional in the classroom and in on-line instruction. It was one of the concerns the AEP faculty raised in their initial discussion at Beavertail. As a result, when they returned to campus, they created critical questions in six areas that would guide them to ensuring that a course created a learning community.

Following these questions are excerpts from the river story showing how Twyla was able to equally apply these same questions in building community with her paddlers.

### Creating a Plan for Building Community

1. **Belonging:**
   What will I do to create a sense of "belonging" at the very start of the course?

   > **Harpham Flats:** "The last thing Twyla did was to take a handful of rubber wrist bands from her bag—the wrist bands were one of Twyla's ways of beginning to build a learning community."

   What will I do to sustain the sense of community throughout the course?

   > **Beavertail:** "I think the most fabulous thing you did, Twyla, was to transform eight head-strong people into a highly functioning community." (PJ Plunkett)

2. **Visioning:**
   How will I share the full picture of the journey we are undertaking together?

   > **The Bus:** Twenty minutes later we rolled to a stop at a place called Sandy Beach—the take-out. It was part of Twyla's plan to show us the finish line before traveling to the put-in at Harpham Flats."

### 3. Engaging:

What activities will I plan that will actively engage them with each other?

**Wapanitia Rapid:** "Twyla taught us the basic paddling skills and commands. I was surprised that Twyla could use just these five phrases to move us through the placid waters at her command:

> FORWARD PADDLE
>
> LEFT PADDLE
>
> RIGHT PADDLE
>
> BACK PADDLE
>
> FORWARD PADDLE, DIG."

In what specific activities will I engage myself as a member of the community?

**Boxcar Rapid:** "But no! Delco was out of the raft.

"It had happened so quickly!

"Twyla called to Sonny to grab Delco. Holding his paddle backwards and reaching far out over the side of the raft he was clearly over-extended. PJ jumped up and held Sonny's life jacket. In seconds Delco was back in the raft. No more than 10 seconds in the water! This was evidence that Twyla and the river had taught us well, both technically and interpersonally. We raised our paddles in a salute to our success, and Twyla whispered to herself, 'No busted boobs this trip!'"

### 4. Caring:

In what different ways will I communicate that I care about them?

**The Boathouse:** As PJ reported, "We lost our guide within the first 15 minutes and found ourselves pinned to a rock in the middle of the river. We were lucky to make it, and I have not been on the river since." Twyla touched his arm and said, "PJ, this isn't the Klickitat; this river is fully predictable. I know this river and you will be safe in my raft."

### 5. Respecting:

What will I do to show respect for all members of our community?

**Box Car Rapid** (after): "Contrary to her concerns about PJ at the put-in, Twyla thought he was ready for the front and she needed his physical strength in that position. His paddling skills were surprisingly stronger than Jennifer's, a necessity for getting through Oak Springs."

### 6. Sharing Responsibility:

What will I do to find out whether members of the community feel that I have carried out my specific responsibilities to the community?

**Harpham Flats:** Twyla turned to us and asked, "Is there something else I need to do for anyone, before we make our final preparations?"

How will I help them understand their own responsibility to themselves and their work teams?

**Wapinitia Rapid:** Twyla called it a *riffle-of-a-rapid*, just big enough to give us a bit of confidence. It illustrated the need to follow her commands and synchronize with Bernie, the lead paddler at the front left. Even this tiny rapid taught us a big lesson: teamwork is not an option. At the same time, we were each having a different experience.

In *Part Three, Community Building Tool*, pages 101–104, you will find an example of how the classroom guide in AEP 212 used the above questions and how you can build a sense of community in your own course(s).

# WATERMARK VI
## Engage with Learners to Build Proficiency

This sixth watermark is what most people think of when they hear the t-words, "I teach." But when we substitute the word *guide* from an outcomes-based curriculum, it takes on more specific meaning. We see two specific concepts in this one Watermark. The first is to engage with students on their journey toward intended outcomes and the second is to build proficiency necessary to achieve the outcomes.

To engage means we devote our attention and effort to the student's progress. On the river, it is clearly obvious that Twyla had to devote her attention and effort to everything that was happening in the raft from put-in to take-out. While the same level of attention might not always be necessary (or even desired) in the classroom setting, it raises an important issue. How much, and in what specific ways, should we directly engage with students in our course? It is a question we all have to ask ourselves, and the answer should be based on student needs.

On-line classes raise a particular concern about faculty engagement. When we are in a face-to-face classroom, it can be assumed that the instructor will at least be present, if not engaged, during class time. In the on-line course, there is reason to believe that instructor engagement with learners becomes increasingly important, but more often falls short. All things considered, this is one of the reasons some colleges work hard to cap enrollment for on-line instruction.

The second major concept embedded in this instructional practice is the focus on building proficiency. In today's culture of accountability, there is a higher expectation of instructors when a course is outcomes driven. While this creates anxiety for some, it shouldn't. It doesn't mean an instructor is solely responsible for students to succeed, but it does mean the instructor is accountable for guiding students toward intended outcomes and assisting them to achieve a defined standard of proficiency.

Instructors, like Twyla on the river, who are particularly effective in building student proficiency, exhibit specific skills. Here are the major ones Twyla exhibited that helped students build proficiency:

**Focus:** the ability to concentrate on what is essential to the intended outcome.

> **Boxcar Rapid:** "Twyla told us we had to do four important things to get safely through Boxcar. 'We'll need to skirt the pillow just under the water's surface, avoid the strainer (fallen trees jutting out from the river's edge), keep up our speed, and hit the tongue. Hitting the tongue, the V-shaped flow into the rapid, will be critical.'"

**Sequence:** the ability to move the student from simple to more complex concepts, issues and skills.

> **Beaver Tail:** Twyla said, "Bernie, the only way we could build proficiency today in both rafting and working together was to start from the simple and work toward the complex tasks."

**Engage:** the ability to involve students in real-life applications and collaborative activity. Getting students engaged hinges on being able to give clear directions. This is one of the major differences between teaching and guiding—"teaching from the front" compared to "guiding from the back."

> **Boxcar Rapid:** "I felt a strong bounce and my body sank deeper into the raft. Twyla used her paddle to move us to the left of the pillow. We glared at the pillow just under the surface and recognized immediately how dangerous it could be. Then it all happened so fast. We brushed the side of a boulder on the left and caught sight of a strainer to the right. Twyla called out
>
> BACK PADDLE
>
> STOP
>
> In a matter of seconds we moved past the fallen tree into shallow, choppy water.

**Dig Deep:** the ability to present problems and pose questions requiring critcal thinking and depth of content.

> **Boxcar Rapid:** In the flat water again, Twyla quizzed us. "What would have happened had Bernie gone into the river on that wave?"

**Monitor:** the ability to probe and provide specific feedback on student progress.

> **Boxcar Rapid:** "After giving us some time to reflect, Twyla pointed out the things she wanted us to fix. Among other things, Delco certainly needed to better secure his feet under the thwarts. Above all we need to continue paying attention to that tongue."

In *Part Three, Proficiency Building Tool*, pages 105–109, you will find a more complete description of the kinds of things the AEP instructors do to build proficiency.

# WATERMARK VII
## Assess to Assist

Throughout the education system, there is a distorted perception that assessment is about assigning a grade, rather than on assessment as an essential part of the learning process. Assessing what students can do at progressive intervals is perhaps the most powerful way to increase learning and performance. It requires the guide's greatest attention.

When we look at Twyla's entire river run from the put-in talk to the Sandy Beach take-out, we see assessment splashing everywhere. Even while the paddlers practiced on flat water between the major rapids, Twyla provided timely feedback based on specific criteria essential to the paddlers' success. The river story tells us loudly that assessing to assist is central to the concept of "guiding".

Each subsequent rapid provided yet another opportunity for Twyla to *assess to assist*.

> After giving us some time to reflect, Twyla pointed out the things she wanted us to fix. Among other things, Delco certainly needed to better secure his feet under the thwarts. Above all we need to continue paying attention to that tongue. Getting into the rapid right would be a key to success and prevent a flip.

Because Twyla was in the raft with the paddlers every mile of the way, it was natural for her to share her expertise at the specific moment it was needed. It can be so different in both the real and the virtual college classroom. With greater numbers of students and less physical proximity, we have to intentionally create both formal and informal ways of observing and assessing progress.

One efficient way to assess to assist, in any proximity, is to provide assessment criteria that is so specific that students themselves can assess their own progress. For every rapid, we simply build the criteria into what we call a *scoring guide*. The scoring guide describes what is "good" work in sufficient detail to be used by the instructor, a peer, or even the student. When we give students clear criteria and feedback while they are learning, rather than holding out for a grade, we greatly increase their chance of being successful. Criteria for good performance should never be a secret.

Scoring guides take many different forms. Figure 2.7 on page 70 shows one example of a partial scoring guide that the faculty developed for one of their major assessment tasks in AEP 212, Alternative Energy Systems. The complete scoring guide is shown in **Part Three, Scoring Guide Tool**, pages 111–14, along with instructions for developing your own scoring guides.

## Scoring Guide: Constructing a Wind Energy System
### (Course Outcome: Use the principles of science to fabricate and test prototypes)

Directions: Self-assess each factor below using the following rating scale:

| 1=absent | 2=minimally met | 3=adequately met | 4=exceptionally met |

## Quality Factors:

**A. Construction and Fabrication** — 1 2 3 4 — Factor Average

| | 1 | 2 | 3 | 4 |
|---|---|---|---|---|
| 1. appropriate use of materials for prototype | | | | |
| 2. electric motor (DC) appropriate for prototype | | | | |
| 3. wiring appropriate for prototype | | | | |
| 4. three sets of wind blades constructed for testing | | | | |

**B. Performance of Prototype** — 1 2 3 4 — Factor Average

| | 1 | 2 | 3 | 4 |
|---|---|---|---|---|
| 5. test directions followed (as per instructor guidelines) | | | | |
| 6. voltmeter appropriate for collecting voltage output | | | | |
| 7. three shapes of blades tested | | | | |
| 8. three angles of blades tested | | | | |
| 9. fan or natural wind speed tested on voltage output | | | | |

**C. Data Collected (Test Prototype)** — 1 2 3 4 — Factor Average

| | 1 | 2 | 3 | 4 |
|---|---|---|---|---|
| 10. blade angle on voltage output at 15° | | | | |
| 11. blade angle on voltage output at 30° | | | | |
| 12. blade angle on voltage output at 45° | | | | |
| 13. blade angle on voltage output at 60° | | | | |
| 14. blade shape #1 on voltage output | | | | |
| 15. blade shape #2 on voltage output | | | | |
| 16. blade shape #3 on voltage output | | | | |
| 17. fan speed (fast) on voltage output | | | | |
| 18. fan speed (medium) on voltage output | | | | |
| 19. fan speed (slow) on voltage output | | | | |

Figure 2.7

Prickel and Stiehl

# WATERMARK VIII
## Assess to Advance

*Assessing to advance* is what most of us think of as "passing" or giving a grade for the course. And it is. It's not about assessing to assist, to help the student along the way. It is about making a judgment on the degree to which they have achieved the intended outcomes for the course.

In the past, evidence to advance has consisted largely of test scores, especially the "final exam." We are getting wiser now. The practice of using written exams might provide evidence of what our students KNOW, but it rarely reveals what they can actually DO with what they know. We are finally learning in higher education that knowing isn't enough! In college classrooms, knowing is never enough to ensure intended outcomes.

The only way Twyla was able to make judgments about the team's advancement to the next rapid was by seeing what they could do. They paddled through that last Oak Springs rapid, and Twyla observed the evidence. They engaged in the conversation at Beavertail, and Jacqueline looked for further evidence. Assessing to advance in the college classroom is formalized through the use of summative rubrics.

A summative rubric is a tool that helps the guide put the student's performance in a category based on quality of the work. It differs somewhat from the scoring guide that can be used for assisting the student.

Figure 2.8 on page 72 shows a partial example of how the summative rubric for AEP 212 was structured for the capstone energy site assessment task. You can see that it is less specific than the scoring guide and most often requires the professional judgment of the instructor.

Developing a good summative rubric takes time, but when done, it is far less time-consuming to use than scoring guides. Primarily used at the end of the course when instructor time is at a premium, rubics are a godsend.

***Part Three, Summative Rubric Tool***, pages 115–18, provides a complete example of the above rubric along with specific guidelines for creating your own.

## Summative Rubric: AEP 212, Alternative Energy System

Name of Student: _____  Date Submitted: _____

Capstone Description: Conduct an energy site assessment

Course #: AEP 212: Alternative Energy Systems                                   Term _____

(Factor Weight: 1=Important   2=Necessary to meet standards   3=Absolutely Essential)

| Factors | 1 Standards NOT Met | 2 Basic Standards Met | 3 Work Commendable | 4 Outstanding Work | Factor Weight 1,2,3 |
|---|---|---|---|---|---|
| **Location of energy site assessment** | Site not well-defined. Does not name the exact location of site assessment | Location of site assessment is identified by type with no details | Site assessment is identified by its exact address, city, and type (house, business, etc.) | Exact address, city, specific type, and rationale for choosing site assessment | 1 |
| **Current fossil fuel in use** | Fossil fuel not mentioned at site | Fossil fuel identified only | Fossil fuel and energy system identified (e.g. coal with furnace) | Fossil fuel and energy system identified, with upgrades and changes (history) noted in detail | 2 |
| **Technical feasibility of proposed alternative energy system** | Lacks any rationale for proposed alternative energy system to replace current system | Argues for benefits or challenges involved in the technical feasibility of proposed alternative energy system, but not both | Argues for the benefits and also notes the challenges involved in the technical feasibility of proposed alternative energy system | Examines both benefits and limitations, and provides convincing arguments why benefits outweigh limitations of proposed alternative energy system | 3 |

Figure 2.8

 # WATERMARK IX
## Gather and Track Learning Evidence

Both on the river and at Beavertail, Twyla and Jacqueline gathered considerable evidence of what the paddling team was able to do with what they learned as a result of the seemingly irrelevant excursion on the river. But there was no need for them to formalize the evidence. This is where we have to leave the river.

Gathering and tracking student learning evidence is the classroom guide's best response to the concerns for accountability in higher education today.

It's no surprise to any of us who work in higher education that our colleges collect and track data on many things, from enrollment figures to budget expenditures and grade point averages. It's part of running the business. But what might surprise us is that colleges are rapidly gearing up to track direct evidence of learning, and for faculty stuck in the old school, it is no easy task. The good news is that if we practice the previous eight Watermarks, only two things remain: 1) to gather up and display the evidence in a format that is useful (Watermark IX) and 2) to adjust our instructional practices (Watermark X).

One of the important distinctions faculty must make in gathering learning evidence is between direct and indirect evidence. Direct evidence comes from a direct scrutiny of student performance through observation, test scores, scoring guides, rubrics, exit interviews, and work samples directly reflecting the intended outcome. Indirect evidence is anything else that might reflect the learning results: self-assessment, peer assessment, completion rates, job placement, and student surveys on a variety of issues.

The most efficient way to track and display learning evidence is through the use of tables and graphs. Learning evidence can easily be generated from both qualitative and quantitative data and revealed through tables and graphs.

In AEP 212, direct evidence of student performance on designing and fabricating a wind energy system for four quality factors is shown on page 74 (Figure 2.9). Scores reveal good-to-high student performances on three of the four quality factors, but students had significant difficulty in analyzing their results when constructing wind energy systems. Such a finding may indicate a need for AEP faculty to adjust their practices based on this evidence (Watermark X).

Indirect evidence of student performance was collected through a number of informal questions. Students were asked how successful they felt they were in this course. The table and Figure 2.10 on page 74 show the indirect evidence collected, based on their responses. Simply, it reveals that the majority of students see themselves succeeding and believing in their own learning efficacy.

*Part Three, Evidence Display Tools*, pages 119–31, illustrates further how useful data gathered from qualitative and quantitative assessment tools can be tracked and displayed graphically for your course.

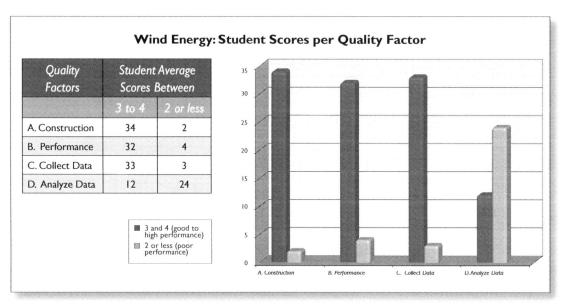

Figure 2.9

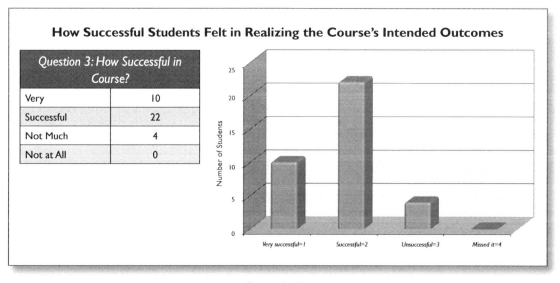

Figure 2.10

# WATERMARK X
## Adjust Practices Based on Evidence

In the epilogue of the river story, Back at the Boathouse, Twyla reviewed the Oak Springs pictures as direct evidence of the intended outcomes for the in-service day. In addition, she thought back over the specific comments the paddlers made at Beavertail concerning the rafting experience. She was taken by what PJ suggested was missing.

What PJ said was:

> "The experience you gave us today was the most perfect in-service I could ever imagine. Using the river was brilliant. There is only one thing I think would have improved it; we needed more eddy-outs. It takes time to absorb all that is happening. For ten whole years, I have been reflecting on what our guide on the Klickitat did so wrong. I suspect I'll be reflecting for a good long time on what you did right. Reflection is powerful, you know. Throw in some more eddies the next time you do this."

Twyla took PJ's feedback seriously and began immediately to think about ways she could adjust the river experience for other educators.

Just like Twyla, most effective college instructors, at the end of the day, contemplate what they can do differently to improve the learning experience for their students. This process of self-adjusting is what we naturally do. Documenting the changes we actually make is something we rarely do. Accreditation standards, today, require documentation at both the program and course level.

Accreditation organizations refer to this instructional practice as "closing the loop"—turning the focus of learning back on ourselves, so that we continuously improve the course and our own performance. Some have gone so far as to say that adopting this practice is the sure sign of a "learning college."

Our challenge, then, is to create a process (and template) for documenting, in a consistent way, the changes we make based on learning evidence. It means systematically reviewing the intended outcomes, the content, the map, the rapids, the environment, the way we build student proficiency, how we assess, and even how we gather evidence.

The AEP 212 faculty created a plan for making course adjustments and changes. A portion of that plan is shown in Figure 2.11 on page 76.

*Part Three, Course Adjustment Planning Tool*, pages 132–42, shows a complete analysis of the AEP 212 course, including all data displays of both direct and indirect learning evidence, identifying the instructor's adjustments and changes to be made when teaching this course the next term. Use this tool to assist you in doing the same process. Suggestions for completing a larger Academic Program Review, as required by most colleges, is found in our companion book, *The Assessment Primer: Creating a Flow of Learning Evidence*.

## Course Adjustment Planning Tool (CAPT)

**Course Title:** <u>AEP 212: Alternative Energy Systems</u>     **Term:** <u>Fall 2011</u>

**Instructor:** <u>Greg Gunderson</u>     **Program:** <u>Alternative Energy Technology</u>

| Quality Indicators | Action Plan for Making Course Changes and Adjustments |
|---|---|
| A. Using the "Student Assessment of Instructor's Performance" and "Instructor's Self-Reflection and Assessment" checklists, examine your performance of the ten Watermarks. List or note any thoughts and key changes you plan to make in your future classroom guiding practices. Write the changes you want to make in the column to the right. | **Safety Glasses:** Review safety procedure and especially the wearing of safety glasses during labs and other work sessions.<br><br>**COG and MAP:** Use these two tools more often and review them consistently, even though, at times, I feel it is a waste of their time, but students say it is not. |
| B. Attach and analyze any evidence displays (tables and graphs) of direct learning evidence (from authentic tasks such as key assessments, capstones, exams, tests) developed from Watermark IX that suggests causes for course changes and/or adjustments. | **Data Analysis:** In all three key assessments, *Quality Factor D: Data Analysis* showed students having trouble explaining the variables and their interacting relationships. I need to add more time in class helping them analyze these variables to build their learning proficiency. |
| C. Attach and analyze any data displays of indirect learning evidence (student observations, informal surveys) developed from Watermark IX that suggests causes for course changes and/or adjustments. | **Students Worked Hard:** As indirect evidence, students reported to me that they worked hard and that the effort was worth the learning they received in return. This confirmed my feeling that I provided them with "good" classroom guiding— seems no changes are needed here. |

Figure 2.11

# Conclusions

These ten Watermarks synthesize our combined 70 years of investigation into college instruction through both research and experience across all levels of higher education. Our challenge has been to boil off the sap (like maple syrup farmers in New England), until we were left with these rich, pure Watermarks.

## Afterthoughts

Might there be an eleventh watermark that the literature overlooks but the river does not? The last words scratched into the dirt at Beavertail was "fun." It raises the question, "What is the place of 'fun' in building a learning community?" Maybe this is our next book!

*What the river says is passionate, but it offers no conclusions. We must each figure out what the river says to us.*

—Rebecca Lawson

# PART THREE

# Tools for Embedding the Watermarks (the rest of the story)

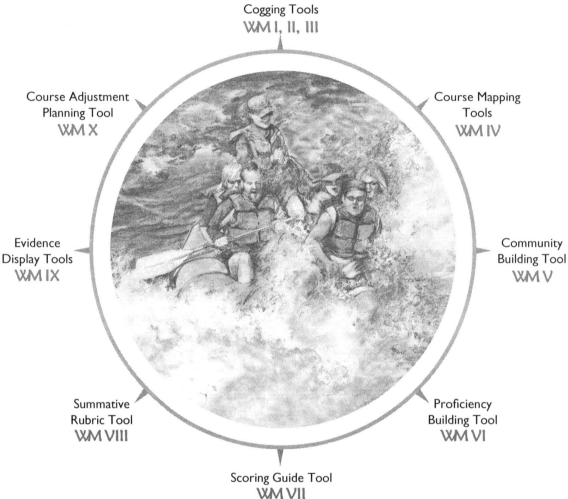

Tools for Embedding the Ten Watermarks

Cogging Tools
WM I, II, III

Course Adjustment
Planning Tool
WM X

Course Mapping
Tools
WM IV

Evidence
Display Tools
WM IX

Community
Building Tool
WM V

Summative
Rubric Tool
WM VIII

Proficiency
Building Tool
WM VI

Scoring Guide Tool
WM VII

of Sound Instructional Practice

As you might recall from the Epilogue in Part 1, before leaving the river, PJ Plunkett told Twyla that he thought the river experience was just a "perfect in-service day." But was it? Did it turn out that the Alternative Energy Program faculty members now work more interdependently? Were they actually able to transition from "teacher on the stage" to "guide at the back"? The only real way to know is to follow the rest of the AEP story.

## Introduction

In Part Three, you will see some of the evidence of what the AEP faculty learned (and continued to learn) about guiding students toward significant outcomes. It didn't all happen in the following week or even the following month; it takes time for any river to sculpt a new landscape.

The first important part of the transition was their identification of the **Ten Watermarks of Sound Instructional Practice** that you reviewed in Part Two. Each of the Watermarks became the focus of their conversations throughout the academic year, until they had developed tools to help them put the Watermarks into practice in each course.

Since the faculty's first conversations were focused around *AEP 212: Alternative Energy Systems*, everything you will find here in Part Three, as evidence of their learning, reflects their work on that course. You will see the tools they developed around each of the ten Watermarks that emerged out of the Beavertail discussion. You will be able to adapt them for your own use.

The AEP faculty were under no illusion. They knew that moving from "teaching" to "guiding" toward significant learning outcomes would require more than participating in a six-hour reality experience on a whitewater river. But they also knew that just thinking of their students as a raft of paddlers, facing new, challenging experiences, would be powerful—mighty powerful.

# Template: Course Outcomes Guide

Course Title: _____    Instructor: _____

Degree/Program: _____    Date Revised: _____

| Concepts and Issues | Skills | Assessment Tasks | Intended Outcomes |
|---|---|---|---|
| Concepts:<br><br><br><br><br><br><br><br><br>Issues: | | | |
| What concepts must students understand? What issues must they resolve? | What skills must students master? | What will students do to demonstrate evidence of outcomes? | What do students need to be able to DO "out there" for which this course is responsible? |

# "COGGING" TOOLS

"COGGING" isn't one of those terms you hear on the river. It's a new course-planning term—meaning the process for collaboratively developing a one-page course plan that results in a *Course Outcomes Guide (COG)*. The COG was introduced in 1995 when outcomes-based learning first became an accreditation standard for higher education. It was first described and published in the ***Outcomes Primer: Reconstructing the College Curriculum*** (See Recommended Readings, page 155).

The AEP faculty chose the "cogging" process to summarize their course outcomes, key assessments, and essential content in a way that provided the entire framework for the course in, literally, one page. Not only that, but their carefully conceived COG addressed three of the most important

Watermarks of sound instructional practice:

WM I    Envision real-life outcomes

WM II    Create energy-generating challenges

WM III    Analyze outcomes for essential content

To construct the framework for AEP 212, the faculty had to do three things: identify the intended learning outcomes, create the challenges, and finally, figure out the essential content—everything suggested by the three Watermarks.

In this section, you will find the COG template (facing page), the collaborative processes they went through for each part of the COG, quality checklists, and their actual one-page COG for Course 212, *Alternative Energy Systems*.

## COGGING OUTCOMES

Learning outcomes are not goals and objectives in new wrappers. Outcome statements describe what students should be able to do outside the classroom—not inside it! They describe what faculty deeply hope students will be able to DO in real life roles for which the instructors have a shared responsibility. Defining, stating, and determining how to assess meaningful learning outcomes is the essence of curriculum planning today. Here is the process the AEP faculty used to collaboratively develop their learning outcomes for AEP 212, and subquently with all their other courses.

## Process for Cogging Learning Outcomes

1. **Invite knowledgeable participants**
   The program coordinator, Jackie, asked three instructors, one field representative, and one upper-division student to participate in developing outcomes for AEP 212. Having multiple perspectives was important.

2. **Prepare materials**
   Jackie taped 3 sheets of flip chart paper to a wall, picked up some 3" by 3" Post-it® notes, and a fine point Sharpie pen for each participant.

3. **Start the Work Session**
   She led the team to identify the kind of real-life role(s) for which this course would begin to prepare students. She listed the roles at the top of the flip charts.

4. **Brainstorm Together**
   Next, Jackie wrote the following question on the flip chart and led the brainstorming: *What do students need to be able to DO "out there" in the rest of life that we are responsible for "in here," in this course?*

   To focus the discussion, Jackie used these rules:

   > **Rule 1.** Begin every answer with an action word—no single word answers (examples: work in teams; analyze the parts; outline a sentence).

   > **Rule 2.** Write each response on a single Post-it® note. Read each answer out loud to all before randomly placing the Post-it® notes onto the flip chart.

   > **Rule 3.** Write as fast as you can, and do not discuss any of the answers until the brainstorming is over.

   It took twenty minutes for the Post-it® notes to emerge, after which Jackie pushed another five minutes for the less obvious answers.

5. **Cluster the Responses**

   Jackie asked the team to silently cluster the ideas (now on Post-it®
   notes) into several thematic categories, then to discuss the clusters
   and make changes before writing a short sentence that best describes the ideas contained within each cluster respectively. **Rule:**
   Be sure to begin each sentence with an appropriate action word.

6. **Refine the Outcome Statements**

   Jackie led the team in the work of refining each of the outcome
   statements until they were certain they had sufficiently answered
   this question: *Does this statement clearly express what we can
   expect our students to be able to do "out there" in the roles we
   have listed above?*

7. **Check the Quality of the Statements**

   To check the strength of their statements, the team used the Scoring Guide: Assessing the Quality of Intended Outcome Statements
   on page 86 to assess the quality of their outcomes for this course.

8. **Capture and Save the Work**

   The instructor of the course offered to edit and finalize the team's work
   by listing all the ideas on the Post-it® notes under the outcome statements. Figure 3.1 on page 87 shows the results of the outcomes work
   session completed by the AEP faculty.

A blank template for documenting the results of your outcomes work sesson
is provided on page 88.

## Template: Scoring Guide—Assessing the Quality of Intended Outcome Statements

| Characteristics of Good Learning Outcome Statements | 1 | 2 | 3 | 4 | Suggestions/ Improvements |
|---|---|---|---|---|---|
| **1. Action** | 1 | 2 | 3 | 4 | |
| All the statements are written in active voice, and the action words have been carefully chosen to describe the intention. | | | | | |
| **2. Context** | 1 | 2 | 3 | 4 | |
| All the statements describe what you envision students doing "after" and "outside" this academic experience—because of this experience. | | | | | |
| **3. Scope** | 1 | 2 | 3 | 4 | |
| Given the time and resources available, the outcome statements represent reasonable expectations for students. | | | | | |
| **4. Complexity** | 1 | 2 | 3 | 4 | |
| The statements, as a whole, have sufficient substance to drive decisions about what students need to learn in this experience. | | | | | |
| **5. Brevity and Clarity** | 1 | 2 | 3 | 4 | |
| The language is concise and clear, easily understood by students and stakeholders. | | | | | |

Adapted from *The Mapping Primer: Tools for Reconstructing the College Curriculum* (see *Recommended Readings*, page 155)

## Results of Outcomes Work Session
## for Course:  <u>AEP 212, Alternative Energy Systems</u>

**Outcomes Statement #1:** *Investigate the technical, economical, and environmental potential (and progress) of new and emerging forms of power generation.*

Identify alternative energies

Explain advantages of an alternative resource

Research resource availability

Calculate the cost benefits and deficits

Analyze impacts on environment

Classify various power systems

Evaluate resource models

List technologies needed for energy systems

Research energy consumption patterns

Compile data

Create visual displays from qualitative and quantitative data

Design presentations.

**Outcomes Statement #2:** *Use the principles of science (basic electricity, mechanics, chemistry, mathematics, and computer technology) to fabricate and test energy prototypes.*

Apply math formulae to solve a problem

Draw schematics of alternative energy systems

Design prototypes with application of physics and chemistry principles

Design prototypes

Build prototypes

Apply principles of electricity to develop prototypes

Work in a team

Clearly communicate thoughts and ideas

Demonstrate prototypes

Demonstrate appropriate mechanical skills in constructing prototypes

**Outcomes Statement #3:** *Follow industry quality and safety procedures for personal gear, equipment, and tools.*

Wear safety gear and eyewear when conducting experiments

Use caution and care when using equipment

Comply with industry-standard safety practices

Use equipment and tools appropriately

Work with care around others

Figure 3.1

## Template:  Results of Outcomes Work Session

**for Course:** _____

**Outcomes Statement**

**#1** _____

Ideas from Post-it® notes

**Outcomes Statement**

**#2** _____

Ideas from Post-it® notes

**Outcomes Statement**

**#3** _____

Ideas from Post-it® notes

(Continue above format if there are more outcome statements)

## COGGING ASSESSMENT TASKS

After carefully defining the learning outcomes for AEP 212, the same team moved on to create the key challenges (assessment tasks) following the process described below:

### Process for Cogging Assessment Tasks (challenges)

1. **Review the Outcomes for the course**
2. **Generate the "rapids"**

   Jackie again led their work by focusing on two specific questions:

   a. *What are some "real-life" challenges that would demonstate proficiency at progressive levels of difficulty leading to outcomes?* (3–4 tasks)

   b. Then she asked the next question. *What can we ask the students to do as a culminating challenge to show evidence of the outcomes?*

   Jackie gave the team three specific guidelines:

   - The first challenge needs to engage students early (see Question **a** above).
   - The middle tasks need to demonstrate on-going mastery of discrete knowledge and skills of content being learned (see Question **a** above).
   - The final task needs to show an integration of the entire learning experience (see Question **b** above).

   Among others, here are the kinds of tasks they initally discussed:

   - design a process or product
   - conduct a project and report out
   - make a presentation
   - explain a solution to a problem
   - compile a portfolio
   - train and/or teach a process
   - model/perform a skill

### 3. Align Assessment Tasks with Outcomes

To make certain their challenges (tasks) aligned with all of the intended outcome statements, Jackie suggested the group put them into the format shown in Figure 3.2 below.

Once in this format, they verified that the Assessment Tasks did in fact align with the Intended Outcomes.

---

**Course Title: <u>AEP 212, Alternative Energy Systems</u>**

| Assessment Tasks | Intended Outcomes |
|---|---|
| 1. Choose an alternative energy system. Write a position paper and speak to the class for 15 minutes on both the pros and the cons of that system from an economics and environmental perspective. (End of third week) | 1. Investigate the technical, economical, and environmental potential (and progress) of new and emerging forms of power generation. |
| 2. As a laboratory team, design and build three simple energy systems: 1) fuel cell, 2) wind, and 3) solar. (Due week 6, 9, and 13 respectively) | 2. Use the principles of science (basic electricity, mechanics, chemistry, mathematics, and computer technology) to fabricate and test energy prototypes. |
| 3. Conduct an energy site assessment and propose an alternative energy solution that includes current system identification, benefits of proposed system, and design/implementation steps for transfer. | 3. Follow industry quality and safety procedures for personal gear, equipment, and tools. |

Figure 3.2

---

In the AEP 212 course, there was one key assessment that came very early, the position paper and presentation. Next came three on-going laboratory experiments, and, finally, a culminating site assessment project at the end. The site assessment task required the integration of content for the entire course.

## COGGING ESSENTIAL CONTENT

The final task in *Cogging* involved identifying the content students would need to learn—the key concepts they'd need to understand, issues they would need to solve, and skills they'd need to develop to demonstrate the intended outcomes.

Here is the process they used to decide on the content for the course.

### Process for Cogging Essential Content

1. **Work Backward from the Outcomes**
   They reviewed both the outcomes and challenges they had already developed.

2. **Look for the Major Concepts**
   Using Post-it® notes and chart paper once again, Jackie had the team post the potential concepts for AEP 212. Concepts are the major ideas studied and developed in the course. Concepts are typically represented by one or two words and often show up in all those Post-it® notes from the outcomes work session. Here are examples of the essential concepts for *AEP 212, Alternative Energy Systems'* outcomes and assessment tasks:

   - renewable energy sources: solar, wind, fuel cells
   - power systems
   - heat transfer
   - thermodynamics
   - kinetic energy

3. **Identify Issues Inherent in the Intended Outcomes**
   Using additional Post-it® notes and a second sheet of paper on the wall, Jackie led them through the identification of issues inherent in the intended outcome statements. Issues denote difficulties or problems that will require a level of critical and analytical thinking. Here are a few examples of issues that students in *AEP 212, Alternative Energy Systems*, will face in demonstrating the outcomes in real-life contexts.

   - Safety of self, community, environment

- System feasibility: technical, economic, environmental
- Return on Investment

4. **Identify the Skill Sets They Must Master**
   To surface the specific skills, students would need to demonstrate the intended outcomes. Jackie simply asked the team what the students must be able to DO that they would achieve primarily through practice and feedback. She cautioned them that skills always begin with action verbs, but they are far more specific and more techical than outcomes statements. Here are some examples of skills that need to be developed in AEP 212.

   - Argue pro and cons of alternative energy over fossil fuel systems
   - Classify key alternative energy resources
   - Analyze existing and proposed alternative energy systems (high-level skill)
   - Fabricate and test prototypes

5. **Self-Assess:**
   Having the team's input on the essential content, the instructor for AEP 212 summarized the content for the course in the one-page *Course Outcomes Guide (COG)* shown in Figure 3.3, page 93. To check the work, the instructor asked these questions:

   a. *If the students understand these concepts and can begin at least to resolve these issues and demonstrate these skills, is there reason to believe they will be able to demonstrate the intended outcomes for the course?*

   b. *Will the assessment tasks, once developed, provide evidence of the intended outcomes?*

   c. *Are there other essential concepts, issues, skills, and tasks that we missed?*

Following the AEP COG, you'll find a scoring guide on page 94 that the AEP faculty adopted to review and assess the quali- ty of their COGs throughout their program.

**Course Outcomes Guide**

**Course Title:** AEP 212, Alternative Energy Systems    **Degree/Program:** Alternative Energy Technology (AAS)

**Date Revised:** Summer 2012    Instructor(s): ........................

| Concepts and Issues | Skills | Assessment Tasks | Intended Outcomes |
|---|---|---|---|
| 1. renewable energy sources: solar, wind, fuel cells<br>2. fossil fuels<br>3. heat transfer<br>4. chemical reaction<br>5. power systems<br>6. energy consumption<br>7. photovoltaic systems<br>8. hydro-electricity<br>9. thermodynamics<br>10. hydrogen systems<br>11. energy quantification<br>12. electrolysis<br>13. PEM (proton exchange membrane)<br>14. convection current<br>15. kinetic energy<br>16. evaluation models<br>17. site assessments<br>Issues:<br>1. safety (self, community, environment)<br>2. feasibility (technical, economic, environmental)<br>3. return on investment | 1. Arguing pros and cons of alternative energy over fossil fuel systems<br>2. Classifying key alternative energy resources according to use, availability, and environmental impact<br>3. Analyzing existing and proposed alternative energy systems related to efficiency, economies, and environment<br>4. Fabricating and testing prototypes<br>5. Using principles of electricity, mechanics, chemistry, mathematics, and science to design/test systems<br>6. Conducting laboratory experiments<br>7. Working safely and using personal protection equipment<br>8. Contributing responsibly to the efforts of a team<br>9. Evaluating energy systems<br>10. Designing feasible solutions to energy problems | 1. Choose an alternative energy system. Write a position paper and speak to the class for 15 minutes on both the pros and the cons of that system from an economics and environmental perspective. (End of third week)<br><br>2. As a laboratory team, design and build three simple energy systems as follows: 1) fuel cell, 2) wind, and 3) solar. (Due week 6, 9, and 13 respectively)<br><br>3. Conduct an energy site assessment and propose an alternative energy solution that includes current system identification, benefits of proposed system, and design/implementation steps for transfer. | 1. Investigate the technical, economical, and environmental potential (and progress) of new and emerging forms of power generation.<br><br>2. Use the principles of science (electricity, mechanics, chemistry, mathematics, computer technology) to fabricate and test energy prototypes.<br><br>3. Follow industry quality and safety procedures for personal gear, equipment, and tools. |
| What must the student understand? | What skills must be mastered? | What will students do to demonstrate evidence of the intended outcomes? | What do students need to be able to DO "out there" for which this course is responsible? |

Figure 3.3

## Template: Scoring Guide—Assessing the Quality of Content and Assessment Descriptions

Use this rating scale to assess how the essential content and assessment tasks align with the course's intended learning outcomes:
1=absent     2=minimally met   3=adequately met   4=exceptionally met

| Characteristics of Good Content Descriptions | 1 | 2 | 3 | 4 | Suggestions for Improvements |
|---|---|---|---|---|---|
| **1. Concepts** | 1 | 2 | 3 | 4 | |
| Consists of key words or phrases that describe the essential ideas about which the students must discover some depth of meaning in order to achieve the intended outcomes (12–20). | | | | | |
| **2. Issues** | 1 | 2 | 3 | 4 | |
| Consists of the key problems students must work to resolve which are inherent in the intended outcomes (3–5). | | | | | |
| **3. Skills** | 1 | 2 | 3 | 4 | |
| Consists of action statements which describe the abilities that are essential to demonstrate the intended outcomes (8–12). | | | | | |
| **4. Assessment Task(s)** | 1 | 2 | 3 | 4 | |
| Consists of short descriptions of meaningful task(s) through which the students can show evidence of their achievement of the intended outcomes (1–4). | | | | | |
| **5. Flow and Continuity** | 1 | 2 | 3 | 4 | |
| When students understand these concepts and issues and develop these skills, they should be able to successfully complete the assessment task(s) which reflect the intended outcomes. | | | | | |
| Course #/Title: _____ | | | | Average score: _____ | |
| Assessed by: _____ | | | | Date Assessed: _____ | |

Adapted from *The Mapping Primer: Tools for Reconstructing the College Curriculum* (see *Recommended Readings*, page 155)

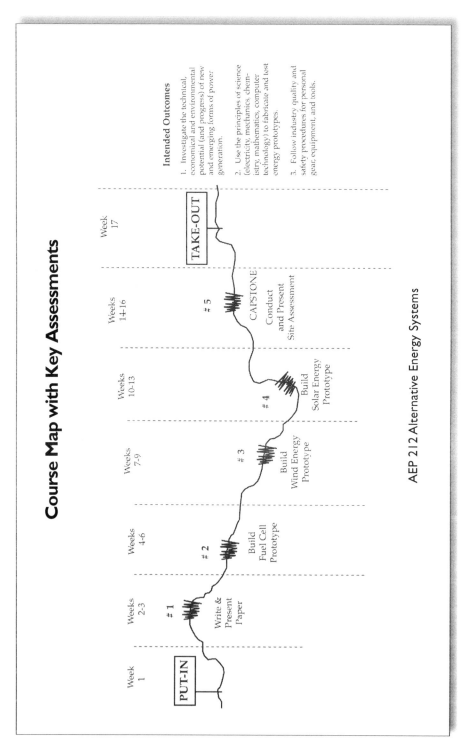

**Course Map with Key Assessments**

Week 1 — PUT-IN

Weeks 2-3 — #1 — Write & Present Paper

Weeks 4-6 — #2 — Build Fuel Cell Prototype

Weeks 7-9 — #3 — Build Wind Energy Prototype

Weeks 10-13 — #4 — Build Solar Energy Prototype

Weeks 14-16 — #5 — CAPSTONE Conduct and Present Site Assessment

Week 17 — TAKE-OUT

**Intended Outcomes**

1. Investigate the technical, economical and environmental potential (and progress) of new and emerging forms of power generation.

2. Use the principles of science (electricity, mechanics, chemistry, mathematics, computer technology) to fabricate and test energy prototypes.

3. Follow industry quality and safety procedures for personal gear, equipment, and tools.

AEP 212 Alternative Energy Systems

Figure 3.4

# COURSE MAPPING TOOLS

Mapping the journey (Watermark IV) means creating and sharing a big picture of what students are likely to experience, put-in to take-out. It can be as simple as a pencil sketch of the "rapids on the river," or as complex as an abstract table of the specific learning activities as they relate to the intended outcomes. No matter the form, the purpose is to focus on the outcome and illustrate how each learning activity will contribute to building proficiency.

When the AEP 212 faculty had their COG in hand, they turned their attention to sequencing the assessment challenges (rapids). They came up with a simple map, built on the river metaphor (Figure 3.4, facing page). Notice that the journey isn't depicted as a straight line, because learning never is. Learning isn't mechanical; it flows like a river flows, and every student's experience takes different turns and creates unique patterns. This meta-image of a course makes it very clear where they are, where they have been, and where they are going in the scope of things.

As the faculty thought more carefully about the content for each section of the river, they also mapped the schedule of learning activities in a table format. Included in these next few pages are 1) *Process for Creating the Course Map*; 2) *Process for Creating an Activity Map*, 3) an example from the AEP 212 course (Figure 3.4, facing page), 4) a blank template (page 99), and 5) the activity map for AEP 212, Alternative Energy Systems, Figure 3.5 on page 100.

## Process for Creating the Course Map (Figure 3.4, facing page)

1. Place vertical dotted lines across the page to represent the number of sessions/weeks in the course. (Notice that on the AEP 212 Map, they combined weeks into clusters).

2. Draw an irregular flowing line across the page representing the natural flow, the ups and downs of learning.

3. Highlight where the key assessments fall. Number and label each, including the capstone.

4. List the course outcomes on the far right at the end of the "flow."

5. Modify the map in any way that you think best provides a mega-image of the students' journey through the course.

## Process for Creating an Activity Map (shown on page 99 and 100)

1. **Create a table with the following features:**

   **Columns:** The AEP faculty designed a table (map) with the number of columns that fit the parameters of the course. They chose to cluster the weeks together.

   **Rows:** For the rows, they identified four major learning activities based on the COG. The most critical row is the bottom, which connects activities to the intended outcomes.

2. **Transfer content from the *Course Outcomes Guide (COG)* onto the *Activity Map*:**

   Notice that they took most of the content from their COG and modified it into a sequence of activities for this type of course map.

   - **Develop a deep understanding of these major concepts:** They asked themselves, "What do we want the students to understand." Generally the answer to this question leads consistently to the "concepts" and "issues" that were earlier identified in forming the COG.

   - **Face these issues:** They asked themselves, "What issues and problems must they be prepared to resolve?"

   - **Master these skills:** Again, they describe these elements in much the same way they do on the one-page COG.

   - **Show Learning Proficiency:** These are the student timelines they set for key assessments.

## Of Special Note:

Notice that the final week of class was devoted to feedback—not testing. "Finals" week, the last week, was devoted to addressing the results of their assessments (or "exams"), gaining evidence for making course adjustments in the future, and simply celebrating the students' successes. So often classes end with final exams and with no opportunity for students to get final feedback and reflect on their failures and successes.

# Template: Course Activity Map    Course: _____    Term: _____

| | Week 1–3 | Week 4–6 | Week 7–9 | Week 10–13 | Week 14–16 | Week 17 |
|---|---|---|---|---|---|---|
| Develop a deep understanding of these major concepts | | | | | | |
| Face these issues | | | | | | |
| Master these skills | | | | | | |
| **Show Learning Proficiency (Key Assessments** | | | | | | |

## Activity Map — AEP 212: Alternative Energy Systems

| | Week 1–3 | Week 4–6 | Week 7–9 | Week 10–13 | Week 14–16 | Week 17 |
|---|---|---|---|---|---|---|
| **Develop a deep understanding of these major concepts** | –history of energy consumption<br>–principles of sciences (mechanics, chemistry, electricity)<br>–electro-chemical reactions<br>–fossil fuels<br>–energy quantification | –fuel cells<br>–electrolysis<br>–PEM (proton exchange membrane)<br>–hydro-electricity<br>–chemical reactions<br>–hydro-electric power generation | –wind energy<br>–wind turbines<br>–thermodynamics<br>–convection current<br>–wind factors: speed & temperature<br>–kinetic energy<br>–distributed energy generation systems | –solar energy<br>–electric connectivity<br>–PV (photovoltaic cells)<br>–modules<br>–arrays<br>–thermal heat/energy<br>–cogeneration | –energy evaluation models<br>–integration of energy systems<br>–site assessments | –feedback from instructor on course assessment tasks and assignments |
| **Face these issues** | –Feasibility: technical, economic, and environmental | –Safety: self, community, and environment | –Laboratory safety<br>–Team relationships | –Return on Investment | –Return on Investment | |
| **Master these skills** | How to:<br>–develop sound arguments for the pros and cons of energy systems<br>–write a good position paper<br>–use statistics to support position on energy systems<br>–contribute equally to work team | How to:<br>–classify energy resources<br>–analyze energy systems<br>–conduct lab experiments<br>–assure safety<br>–contribute to work of the team | How to:<br>–fabricate and test wind turbine prototype<br>–analyze "return on investment" of wind energy systems<br>–conduct lab experiments<br>–interact positively and safely with lab partners | How to:<br>–critically evaluate a solar energy system<br>–observe/examine/record findings of heat loss<br>–design feasible solutions to energy problems | How to:<br>–accept feedback<br>–plan and organize a site assessment<br>–compile quantitative, qualitative analyses<br>–write a report<br>–conduct energy assessments and interpret energy uses | How to:<br>–self-assess performance<br>–give peer and instructor feedback<br>–make adjustments in learning<br>–apply learning to one's personal life situation |
| **Show Learning Proficiency (Key Assessments)** | –Submit position paper of an energy system and make a 15-minute presentation (wk. 3) | –Build prototype of fuel cell system (wk. 6) | –Build prototype of wind energy system (wk. 9) | –Build prototype of solar energy system (wk. 13) | –Develop report & presentation of energy site assessment with proposed solutions (wk. 16) | –Complete course evaluation |

Figure 3.5

# COMMUNITY BUILDING TOOL

Creating a sense of safety, trust, and support was critical to Twyla and her paddlers' navigation through the rapids. Creating this sense of community is an equally important Watermark of sound instructional practice in higher education. Research has verified over and again that the issues of respect, support, safety, and relationships directly affect learning. The question is, "How do you create this kind of learning environment?"

In Part Two, you had a glimpse of a set of questions that the Alternative Energy program faculty developed to help them intentionally build and sustain a sense of community in their courses. On the following pages, you will find their full set of questions (Figures 3.6a–c) as well as how they responded to six characteristics for building a learning community:

- belonging
- visioning
- engaging
- caring
- respecting
- sharing responsibility

---

### Community Building Tool

**Directions:** In preparing for a specific course, reflect on the following questions and document the specific things you plan to do during the course in the interest of establishing a sense of community.

#### BELONGING

| Question: | Notes for AEP 212: |
|---|---|
| What will I do to create a sense of belonging at the very start of my course? | *Conduct a "warm-up" team activity—identify what they know or think they know: what they need or want to know about alternative energy systems.* *Ask a student to help write the ideas on a flip chart.* |
| **Questions:** What will I do to sustain the sense of community throughout the course? | *Have students work in teams on class projects, demonstrate their work, and assist in class preparations.* |

Figure 3.6a

---

## VISIONING

| Question: | Notes for AEP 212: |
|---|---|
| How will I share the full picture of the journey we are undertaking together? | *Share the COG and Course Map in the first class session, and review weekly throughout the course.* |

## ENGAGING

| Question: | Notes for AEP 212: |
|---|---|
| What activities will I plan that will actively engage them with each other? | *In teams of three, I will have students conduct lab experiments together across three main areas: wind, solar, and fuel cells, learning and problem-solving the issues and addressing a set of questions posed. Teams will change with every change of energy system.* |
| Questions: In what specific activities will I engage myself as a member of the community? | *Model and demonstrate each lab experiment before them (for the three areas above) prior to students engaging in the actual lab experiments; observe and pose issues to students during their lab experiments; allow time for practice and review in class.* |

## CARING

| Question: | Notes for AEP 212: |
|---|---|
| In what different ways will I communicate that I care about them? | *Acknowledge (praise) successes and improvements on student performance.*<br><br>*Welcome students as they enter and depart from class sessions.*<br><br>*Offer opportunities for students to submit "drafts" of required projects and tasks prior to final submission; provide timely feedback.* |

Figure 3.6b

## RESPECTING

| Question: | Notes for AEP 212: |
|---|---|
| What will I do to show respect for all members of our community? | *Encourage creativity and diversity when completing tasks as appropriate to the intended outcomes.*<br><br>*Use scoring guides (with clear criteria) to assess objectively and fairly.* |

## SHARING RESPONSIBILITY

| Question: | Notes for AEP 212: |
|---|---|
| What will I do to find out if members of the community feel I have carried out my specific responsibilities to them? | *After each key assessment task, ask them if I could have assisted them in some better way.*<br><br>*Have students complete learner satisfaction surveys about my performance as a classroom guide.* |
| Questions:<br>How will I help them understand their own responsibility to themselves and their work teams? | *Discuss joint responsibility for outcomes.*<br><br>*Assist in assigning roles to each member of a team.* |

Figure 3.6c

This tool shows examples of the faculty's responses to each question in the introductory course, *AEP 212 Alternative Energy Systems*. Both the questions and their responses should help you reflect on how to create and sustain a sense of community in your real or virtual classroom.

## Template: Community Building Tool

**Directions:** In preparing for a specific course, reflect on the following questions and document the specific things you plan to do during the course in the interest of establishing a sense of community.

### BELONGING

| | |
|---|---|
| **Question:** What will I do to create a sense of belonging at the very start of my course? | |
| **Questions:** What will I do to sustain the sense of community throughout the course? | |

### VISIONING

| | |
|---|---|
| **Question:** How will I share the full picture of the journey we are undertaking together? | |

### ENGAGING

| | |
|---|---|
| **Question:** What activities will I plan that will actively engage them with each other? | |
| **Questions:** In what specific activities will I engage myself as a member of the community? | |

### CARING

| | |
|---|---|
| **Question:** In what different ways will I communicate that I care about them? | |

### RESPECTING

| | |
|---|---|
| **Question:** What will I do to show respect for all members of our community? | |

### SHARING RESPONSIBILITY

| | |
|---|---|
| **Question:** What will I do to find out if members of the community feel I have carried out my specific responsibilities to them? | |
| **Questions:** How will I help them understand their own responsibility to themselves and their work teams? | |

# PROFICIENCY BUILDING TOOL

In building proficiency, engagement is everything! Everyone in the learning community—paddlers and guides alike—are equally engaged.

As we might expect, engaging with learners to build proficiency is a good deal more difficult than covering content and assumes greater accountability on both the part of the student and the instructor.

In discussing how to build content proficiency, the AEP faculty settled on five practices they thought were most important in affecting the way students would become proficient. Their intention was to focus on and monitor their own performance on these practices:

> **Focus:** concentrating on what is essential to the intended outcome(s).
>
> **Sequence:** moving with students from simple to more complex concepts, issues, and skills.
>
> **Engage:** involving students in real-life applications and collaborative activity.
>
> **Dig Deep:** presenting problems and posing questions.
>
> **Monitor:** probing and providing specific feedback on student progress.

The AEP faculty created a reflection tool (Figure 3.7a–b on pages 106–7) that helped them consider each of these factors in preparation for each course. While there are other factors that might be equally important, these are the standards they set for themselves. A blank Proficiency Building Tool is provided on pages 108–9 to help you build content proficiency in your own course.

| Proficiency Building Tool | |
|---|---|
| **Building Proficiency** | **What will I do to engage learners to build content proficiency in my course?** |
| 1. **FOCUS:** Concentrate on content that is essential to the intended outcome. | **Notes for AEP 212:**<br><br>*Focus on these intended outcome(s):*<br><br>*1) Investigate the technical, economic, and environmental potentials (and progress) of new and emerging aspects of wind power generation;*<br><br>*2) Use the principles of science (electricity, physics, mechanics, chemistry, mathematics, and computers) to fabricate and test prototypes; and*<br><br>*3) Exercise safe practices and procedures. Focus on these key concepts, issues, and skills—concepts: thermodynamics, convection currents, kinetic energy, speed, temperature; issues: wind speed, blade design, blade angle; and skills: fabricate and test wind prototypes, safety in lab, teamwork.* |

| 2. **SEQUENCE:** Progress from simple understanding to more complex applications of content. | | *Simple* | *Complex* |
|---|---|---|---|
| | *Concepts* | *Define energy, electricity, and wind variables* | *Explain examples of kinetic energy, convection currents, AC & DC current* |
| | *Skills* | *Classify wind energy resources* | *Fabricate and test a wind energy system of one's own design* |
| | *Issues* | *Recognize safety issues in lab* | *Test a system for efficiency and environmental safety* |

| 3. **ENGAGE:** Involve students in real-life applications and collaborative activity. Give clear directions. | *Give students written and oral directions for what we ask them to do.*<br><br>*Organize the lab environment with job aids for the experiments.*<br><br>*Demonstrate processes; observe student work.*<br><br>*Adjust variables to keep students engaged.* |
|---|---|

Figure 3.7a

| Proficiency Building Tool | |
| --- | --- |
| **Building Proficiency** | **What will I do to engage learners to build content proficiency in my course?** |
| 4. **DIG DEEP:** Present problems and pose questions. | *Pose three sets of questions that require student teams to analyze the data they collected, and arrive at answers and solutions. Example:*<br><br>*1. Which angle of the blade produced the highest voltage? Support your answer based on data collected.*<br><br>*2. Which of your team's designs produced the highest voltage? What variable contributed to the higher voltage? Sketch your design and record its dimensions.*<br><br>*3. What is the appropriate relationship between wind speed (fan setting) and voltage? Did increasing the fan speed increase the voltage output of your generator?* |
| 5. **MONITOR:** Probe and provide specific feedback on student progress. | *Teams gather together to share their findings and responses to the above questions. Instructor provides feedback and offers ways for improving each team's performances and findings.* |

Figure 3.7b

## Template: Proficiency Building Tool

| Building Proficiency | What will I do to engage learners to build content proficiency in my course? |
|---|---|
| **1. FOCUS:** Concentrate on content that is essential to the intended outcome. | |
| **2. SEQUENCE:** Progress from simple understanding to more complex applications of content. | *(table below)* |
| **3. ENGAGE:** Involve students in real-life applications and collaborative activity. Give clear directions. | |

|  | Simple | Complex |
|---|---|---|
| *Concepts* | | |
| *Skills* | | |
| *Issues* | | |

## Template: Proficiency Building Tool

| Building Proficiency | What will I do to engage learners to build content proficiency in my course? |
| --- | --- |
| 4. **DIG DEEP:** Present problems and pose questions. | |
| 5. **MONITOR:** Probe and provide specific feedback on student progress. | |

# SCORING GUIDE TOOL

As you recall from Part Two, assessment is so ubiquitous in learning that it has to be thought about in several ways. The AEP faculty chose to think about it in three ways: *assess to assist, assess to advance,* and *assess to adjust.*

Watermark VII, *Assess to Assist,* refers to the on-going instructor observation and feedback from the put-in to the take-out. However, when an instructor creates a scoring guide that explicitly describes the expectations, students can assess themselves and assess to assist their peers. The key here is the robustness of the scoring guide. It must provide, in sufficient detail, the qualities for which the student and guide should be looking.

Good scoring guides are a godsend, for both students and instructors, because nothing is hidden. All the criteria for good performance are shared by everyone in the interest of fairness, consistency, and the improvement of performance. Since implementing the use of scoring guides in the AEP Program, student complaints about "grades" have greatly reduced.

The AEP faculty found that it wasn't necessary to spend long hours developing criteria for each assessment task. In fact, they found that it was impossible to develop the perfect scoring guide on first draft, so they used a process for rapidly prototyping assessment criteria for the scoring guide and then immediately field testing it. Many changes were made during the first several applications of the criteria. Here is the process they settled on for developing the factors and quality indicators that describe to the student "what's good." This process works well, both alone and collaboratively, with other instructors and even with students.

On the next several pages you will find 1) a short description of the collaborative process they used to develop the criteria, 2) the actual scoring guide they developed for one of the key assessment tasks in AEP 212 (Figure 3.8 on page 113), and 3) a scoring guide template you can reproduce.

## Process for Creating a Scoring Guide

1. **Gather Materials:** Large sheet of flip chart paper, packet of 3x3 Post-it® Notes, and a fine-point Sharpie.

2. **Identify one of your assessment tasks**
   Write the assessment task description at the top of your flip chart sheet.

3. **Brainstorm**

Write the question ***What's Good?*** under the assessment task.

Brainstorm and write ideas on separate Post-it® Notes—everything you will look for in the students' performances of this task.

Place the Post-it® Notes randomly on the flip chart paper.

Keep going until you have all the important criteria that should be applied to the work.

4. **Cluster and Chunk**

Look at your Post-it® Notes for commonalities of ideas.

Move the notes around on the chart until you form a number of clusters and/or categories that seem to fit together.

Circle each cluster of notes and label with a word that describes what they have in common.

5. **Review Others' Criteria**

Look to reliable sources to validate your criteria.

Ask colleagues and students their thoughts on "what's good?"

Merge other ideas with your own work.

6. **Triangulate the Results**

Re-cluster all input from Steps 2, 3, and 4.

7. **Convert Results into a Scoring Guide**

Adapt the template to meet your needs, including changing the scale, if necessary.

Use your cluster themes as the major factors (headings).

Draw from your Post-It® Notes to create the indicators under each factor.

**Note:** Use only those statements that are clearly defined and help delineate the major factor.

## Resources for Assessment Tools:

The tools in this book are simple examples with limited explanations. For more work on assessment tools, go to *The Assessment Primer: Creating a Flow of Learner Evidence*, 2008 by Stiehl, R. and Lewchuk, L., available from *www.outcomesnet.com.*

Prickel and Stiehl

## Scoring Guide: Constructing a Wind Energy System
(Course Outcome: Use the principles of science to fabricate and test prototypes.)

Directions: Self-assess each factor below using the following rating scale:
1=absent　　2=minimally met　　3=adequately met　　4=exceptionally met

## Quality Factors

### Ratings

| A. Construction and Fabrication | 1 | 2 | 3 | 4 | Factor Average |
|---|---|---|---|---|---|
| 1. appropriate use of materials for prototype | | | | | |
| 2. electric motor (DC) appropriate | | | | | |
| 3. wiring appropriate | | | | | |
| 4. three sets of wind blades | | | | | |

| B. Performance of Prototype | 1 | 2 | 3 | 4 | Factor Average |
|---|---|---|---|---|---|
| 5. directions followed (as per instructor guidelines) | | | | | |
| 6. voltmeter appropriate | | | | | |
| 7. three shapes of blades tested | | | | | |
| 8. three angles of blades tested | | | | | |
| 9. fan or natural wind speed tested | | | | | |

| C. Data Collected (Test Prototype) | 1 | 2 | 3 | 4 | Factor Average |
|---|---|---|---|---|---|
| 10. blade angle on voltage output at 15° | | | | | |
| 11. blade angle on voltage output at 30° | | | | | |
| 12. blade angle on voltage output at 45° | | | | | |
| 13. blade angle on voltage output at 60° | | | | | |
| 14. blade shape #1 on voltage output | | | | | |
| 15. blade shape #2 on voltage output | | | | | |
| 16. blade shape #3 on voltage output | | | | | |
| 17. fan speed (fast) on voltage output | | | | | |
| 18. fan speed (medium) on voltage output | | | | | |
| 19. fan speed (slow) on voltage output | | | | | |

| D. Data Analysis and Report | 1 | 2 | 3 | 4 | Factor Average |
|---|---|---|---|---|---|
| 20. data is appropriately and accurately graphed for blade angle | | | | | |
| 21. data is appropriately and accurately graphed for blade shape | | | | | |
| 22. data is appropriately and accurately graphed for fan speed | | | | | |
| 23. explains which blade angle produces greatest output | | | | | |
| 24. explains what variables contribute to higher voltage output based on blade design | | | | | |
| 25. identifies the relationship between speed of wind and voltage output | | | | | |

Check one: ____ Self-assessment _____
____ Peer Assessment by _____
____ Instructor Assessment by _____

Average Score: _____
Standard: Average 3.0 or higher; no factor less than 2

Figure 3.8

## Template: Scoring Guide

Student Name: _____ Date: _____

Course Title & #: _____

Task being assessed: _____

Course Outcomes that align with Task: _____

Directions: Self-assess each factor below using the following rating scale:

     1=absent     2=minimally met     3=adequately met     4=exceptionally met

Quality Factors (with indicators)          (Rating Scale)

A. _____

| | Rating | | | | |
|---|---|---|---|---|---|
| 1. _____ | 1 | 2 | 3 | 4 | Factor Average |
| 2. _____ | 1 | 2 | 3 | 4 | |
| 3. _____ | 1 | 2 | 3 | 4 | |
| 4. _____ | 1 | 2 | 3 | 4 | |
| 5. _____ | 1 | 2 | 3 | 4 | |

B. _____

| | Rating | | | | |
|---|---|---|---|---|---|
| 6. _____ | 1 | 2 | 3 | 4 | Factor Average |
| 7. _____ | 1 | 2 | 3 | 4 | |
| 8. _____ | 1 | 2 | 3 | 4 | |
| 9. _____ | 1 | 2 | 3 | 4 | |
| 10. _____ | 1 | 2 | 3 | 4 | |

C. _____

| | Rating | | | | |
|---|---|---|---|---|---|
| 11. _____ | 1 | 2 | 3 | 4 | Factor Average |
| 12. _____ | 1 | 2 | 3 | 4 | |
| 13. _____ | 1 | 2 | 3 | 4 | |
| 14. _____ | 1 | 2 | 3 | 4 | |

D. _____

| | Rating | | | | |
|---|---|---|---|---|---|
| 15. _____ | 1 | 2 | 3 | 4 | Factor Average |
| 16. _____ | 1 | 2 | 3 | 4 | |
| 17. _____ | 1 | 2 | 3 | 4 | |
| 18. _____ | 1 | 2 | 3 | 4 | |

E. _____

| | Rating | | | | |
|---|---|---|---|---|---|
| 19. _____ | 1 | 2 | 3 | 4 | Factor Average |
| 20. _____ | 1 | 2 | 3 | 4 | |
| 21. _____ | 1 | 2 | 3 | 4 | |
| 22. _____ | 1 | 2 | 3 | 4 | |

Check one: ___ Self-assessment _____
          ___ Peer Assessment by _____
          ___ Instructor Assessment by _____

Average Score: _____
Standard: Average 3.0 or higher; no factor less than 2

Comments/Feedback: _____

_____

# SUMMATIVE RUBRIC TOOL

In *AEP 212, Alternative Energy Systems*, the classroom guide asked the students to build and test three prototypes of alternative energy: solar, wind, and fuel cells. The instructor prepared and used a scoring guide with each of the tasks. But assessing to advance (Watermark VIII) needed a different tool for the final capstone requiring students to conduct an energy site assessment—the *Summative Rubric*.

When an instructor assesses to advance the student just before the take-out, a summative rubric is the tool of choice. It is distinguished from a scoring guide in that it is less detailed, more holistic, and often requires little more than circling a category that best describes the quality of a student's performance. Here are five major characteristics of a good summative rubric:

## A Summative Rubric

1. Is holistic rather than reduced to detailed indicators.
2. Synthesizes the criteria from scoring guides used for assisting the student.
3. Enables instructors to make consistent professional judgments based on the same major factors.
4. Saves instructor time in assessing complex work samples.
5. Converts easily to a traditional grading system.

In the next few pages, you will find the following: 1) a short explanation of the process they used to develop their captone rubric, 2) the actual rubric the faculty developed for the AEP 212 capstone assessment task (Figure 3.9 on page 117), and 3) a basic template for developing a rubric (page 118).

### Process for Creating a Rubric

1. **Examine the Scoring Guides:** The lead instructor for AEP 212 looked at the scoring guides they had previously completed for each of the successive tasks. With these in mind, the classroom guide began to consider which should flow over into the final rubric.

2. **Create the template:** A basic rubric template was created, consisting of the major components shown on page 117.

3. **Key Factors:** Looking at both the scoring guides and the final assessment task, the AEP instructor began to identify the major quality factors that described what was expected in this capstone task—the standards that had been communicated throughout the course.

4. **Write the Descriptions:** AEP faculty found this to be the hard part! For each of the factors, the classroom guide worked to describe in as few words as possible what was meant by "not met," "standard met," "work commendable," and "outstanding" as they relate to this one factor. With the help of other faculty, the AEP instructor wrote and rewrote until statements were clearly differentiating.

5. **Solicit Feedback:** Once again, he realized that setting standards isn't just a matter of one person's ideas. The classroom guide tried to substantiate the standard using professional literature and sought feedback from colleagues and students. Still, once the rubric was in use, changes continued to be made in the clarity of the statements.

6. **Field Test Your Rubric:** The rubric used in AEP 212 was field tested during fall semester. It was found that some of the initial factor titles and rating descriptions were too general, vague and even confusing. Changes and modifications were made until clarity of each quality factor was attained, as shown in the summative rubric (Figure 3.9, page 117).

## Summative Rubric: AEP 212, Alternative Energy System

Name of Student_____  Term _____

Capstone Description: <u>Conduct Energy Site Assessment</u>

(Factor Weight: 1=Important   2=Necessary to meet standards   3=Absolutely Essential)

| Factors | 1<br>Standards NOT Met | 2<br>Basic Standards Met | 3<br>Work Commendable | 4<br>Outstanding Work | Factor<br>Weight 1,2,3 |
|---|---|---|---|---|---|
| **Location of energy site assessment** | Site not well-defined. Does not name the exact location of site assessment | Location of site assessment is identified by type with no details | Site assessment is identified by its exact address, city, and type (house, business, etc.) | Exact address, city, specific type, and rationale for choosing site assessment | 1 |
| **Current fossil fuel in use** | Fossil fuel not mentioned at site | Fossil fuel identified only | Fossil fuel and energy system identified (e.g. coal with furnace) | Fossil fuel and energy system identified, with upgrades and changes (history) noted in detail | 2 |
| **Technical feasibility of proposed alternative energy system** | Lacks any rationale for proposed alternative energy system to replace current system | Argues for benefits or challenges involved in the technical feasibility of proposed alternative energy system, but not both | Argues for the benefits and also notes the challenges involved in the technical feasibility of proposed alternative energy system | Examines both benefits and limitations, and provides convincing arguments why benefits outweigh limitations of proposed alternative energy system | 3 |
| **Environmental impact of proposed alternative energy system** | Lacks any rationale, or reasons are illogical for the environmental impacts of proposed alternative energy system | Identifies subjectively some positive environmental impacts in the use of the proposed alternative energy system, but lacks data and references to support one's claims | Identifies a number of positive environmental results in the use of the proposed alternative energy system, and justifies these with current data and references to support the claims | Compares the positive and negative environmental impacts between current fossil fuel usage and the proposed alternative energy system.; uses current data and research evidence to justify the proposed alternative energy system as being more environmentally friendly | 3 |
| **Return on Investment (ROI) of energy system** | Lacks any reference to an ROI or calculations are inaccurate or inappropriate | Provides only a quantitative ROI analysis of proposed alternative energy system | Calculates either a positive or negative ROI of proposed energy system; calculations are vague | Provides both a quantitative and a qualitative ROI analysis of proposed alternative energy system | 2 |

Average Score: _____  (Any factor score of "1" results in course failure)

Comments: _____
_____

Instructor Name:_____  Date Assessed: _____

Figure 3.9

# Template: Summative Rubric Tool

Name of Student _____ Term _____

Capstone Description: _____

(Factor Weight: 1=Important   2=Necessary to meet standards   3=Absolutely Essential

| Factors | 1<br>Standards NOT Met | 2<br>Basic Standards Met | 3<br>Work Commendable | 4<br>Outstanding Work | Factor<br>Weight 1,2,3 |
|---|---|---|---|---|---|
|  |  |  |  |  |  |
|  |  |  |  |  |  |
|  |  |  |  |  |  |
|  |  |  |  |  |  |
|  |  |  |  |  |  |

Average Score: _____ (Any factor score of "1" results in course failure)

Comments: _____

Instructor Name: _____ Date Assessed: _____

# EVIDENCE DISPLAY TOOLS

In contrast to the past practices, it is no longer enough to just assign and give letter grades to students. To some instructors, this might come as a surprise. Accreditation standards now require that colleges track and display evidence of student performance in far more detail. The reason is not so much that someone is asking for more proof; it's that we need evidence that will help us to improve our own performance.

As discussed in *Part Two, Watermark IX*, there are two kinds of evidence the AEP faculty began to track: direct evidence and indirect evidence of the outcomes. When they used scoring guides and rubrics, they were collecting direct evidence of student perfor-

mance. However, they used several other means of collecting data about such things as how students felt about different aspects of the experience—data that had bearing on their performance, but were not a direct measure. Both direct and indirect evidence can be quite easily quantified and then displayed in tables and graphs for easy analysis.

In the following pages, we show how the AEP 212 faculty converted direct evidence from scoring guides and rubrics into tables and graphs, as well as data from student surveys which provided important indirect evidence. We include the processes they used for creating and analyzing the graphs.

## DISPLAYING DIRECT LEARNING EVIDENCE

The AEP faculty chose one of the key assessment tasks for AEP 212 to experiment with displaying data. The one they chose was, "construct/build a wind energy system," for which they had earlier constructed the criteria, scoring guide, and generated data. You will find this scoring guide on page 113.

Here is the process the AEP faculty used to create useful graphs from the data.

### Tabulate Overall Scores—A Macro-View:

To obtain a "big picture" of student performance, the faculty first totaled the overall scores from the students' scoring guides of key assessments for the entire AEP 212

course. Using Excel, the computer produced two simple graphs. First, the faculty compiled the final and total scores of students' performances in AEP 212, as shown in the table below and in Graph 3.1, page 120. Then they wanted to see a more detailed comparison of students' performance across three key assessments as shown in the table on page 120 and Graph 3.2, page 121.

| Scores | Number of Students |
|---|---|
| 92–100 pts | 18 |
| 80–91 pts | 10 |
| 70–79 pts | 7 |
| 1–69 pts | 1 |

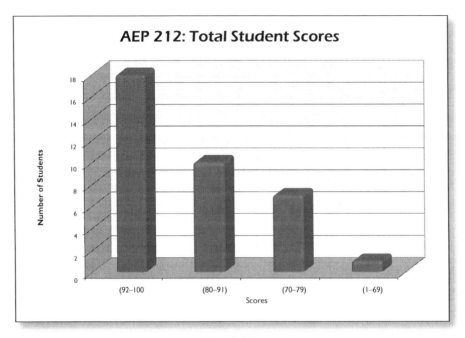

Graph 3.1

Student scores on all the three key assessments were also collected for a more in-depth, macro-view analysis.

## Students Scores: Three Key Assessments

| Scores | Wind | Solar | Fuel Cell |
|---|---|---|---|
| (92–100 pts) | 18 | 12 | 22 |
| (80–91 pts) | 10 | 13 | 10 |
| (70–79 pts) | 7 | 10 | 4 |
| (1–69 pts) | 1 | 1 | 0 |

(Converted to a graph on page 121)

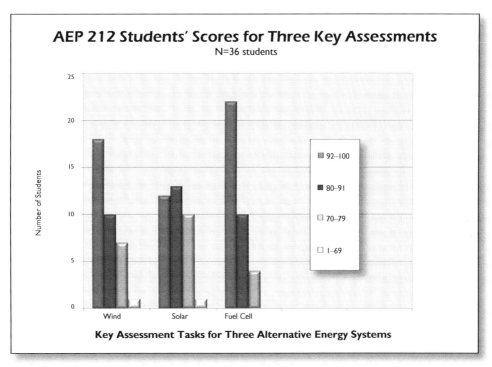

Graph 3.2

On first analysis, the above results indicate a high level of student mastery and achievment of the intended outcomes. A deeper analysis shows a number of students with scores below 80 which led them to further investigate the quality factors of each key assessment.

## Tabulate Factor Averages:

They compiled the number of students who scored ratings of 3 and 4 (good/exceptional performance) and ratings of 1 and 2 (poor performance) for each of the four quality factors (*See Scoring Guide: Constructing a Wind Energy System*, page 113). The results are shown in the table to the right and in the graph on the following page, revealing high factor averages for the first three quality factors of construction/fabrication, performance, and collecting data. It also shows that two students out of every three (two-thirds) faced difficulty and significant challenges in analyzing data in Graph 3.3 on page 122.

| Quality Factors | Student Average Scores | |
|---|---|---|
| | 3–4 | 2 or Less |
| A. Construction | 34 | 2 |
| B. Performance | 32 | 4 |
| C. Collect Data | 33 | 3 |
| D. Analyze Data | 12 | 24 |

(converted to a graph on page 122)

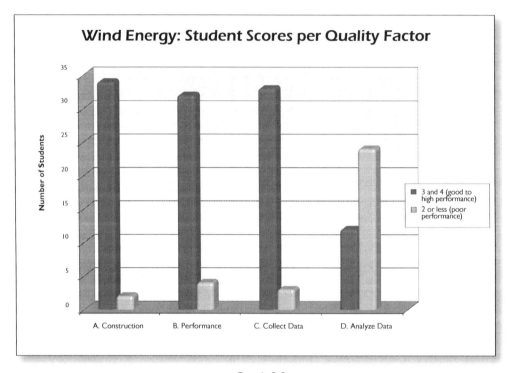

Graph 3.3

## Look more deeply—A Micro-View:

To look more closely at the evidence that revealed students' difficulty with Quality Factor #4: D. Analyze Data, they generated the following table and Graph 3.4 (page 123). The analysis consisted of examining more closely the indicators for this quality factor.

While relative difficulties were shown in graphing the data, as shown in the table and Graph 3.4 on page 123 (items 20–22), the students faced greater challenges with explaining variable effects on voltage outputs (questions 23 and 24), and relationships among variables (question 25). You will see how this data was helpful to them in making course adjustments in the next section.

| Activity Required | Quality Indicator | Between 3–4 | Between 1–2 |
|---|---|---|---|
| Data is appropriately and accurately graphed for blade angle. | 20 | 18 | 18 |
| Data is appropriately and accurately graphed for blade shape | 21 | 21 | 15 |
| Data is appropriately and accurately graphed for fan speed | 22 | 12 | 24 |
| Explains which blade angle produces greatest output | 23 | 10 | 26 |
| Explains what variables contribute to higher voltage output based on blade design | 24 | 6 | 30 |
| Identifies the relationship between speed of wind and voltage output | 25 | 12 | 24 |

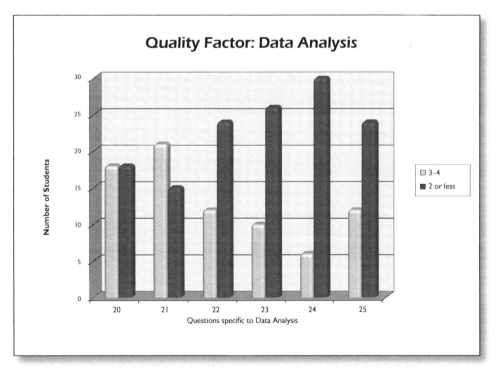

Graph 3.4

## DISPLAYING INDIRECT LEARNING EVIDENCE

The AEP faculty decided to use several different kinds of tools to collect information from students regarding the learning experiences they were going through. They considered the data as important, but indirect. Several of the tools were used at different points during the course, while others were completed near the end.

Based on research regarding the impor-tance of "student self-satisfaction" to learning success, they chose to use an indirect tool for detecting how satisfied students were with their own accomplishment in the course. They collected the information following the key assessment task of "building a wind energy system" at the end of Week 9. Here is the tool they chose to use:

---

### Learner Satisfaction Tool

**Name** (optional): _____  **Date:** _____

**Time Period:** Weeks 7–9     **Student Learning Outcome:** Build a Wind Energy System

**Directions:** Reflect on the following questons and circle one of the given descriptions of how satisfied you are with your learning.

---

**Question 1:** How much effort did you put into this challenge?

| 1 | 2 | 3 | 4 |
|---|---|---|---|
| Gave no effort | Made small effort | Worked at it | Worked hard at it |

---

**Question 2:** To what degree do you feel you were responsible for what you learned and achieved?

| 1 | 2 | 3 | 4 |
|---|---|---|---|
| Sombody else's; not responsible | I had some responsibility | I was responsible | I did it; nobody else |

---

**Question 3:** How successful do you feel you were in realizing the intended learning outcomes for this assessment task?

| 1 | 2 | 3 | 4 |
|---|---|---|---|
| Not at all | Little success | Successful | Very successful |

---

**Question 4:** How much personal satisfaction do you feel from what you have learned or accomplished in this task?

| 1 | 2 | 3 | 4 | 5 |
|---|---|---|---|---|
| Absolutely none | Very little | Some | Quite a bit | Enormous |

---

Adapted from *The Assessment Primer* by Stiehl and Lewchuck, 2008

Figure 3.10

## Tabulate Overall Scores—A Macro-View:

The use of the above tool in *AEP 212, Alternative Energy Systems*, revealed the following results. As seen in the table and Graph 3.5 below, as a whole, students in AEP 212 be- lieved that they expended a lot of effort in this course, or at least up to Week 9, when studying wind energy systems.

| Question 1: Effort Expended in Course AEP212 | |
|---|---|
| No effort | 0 |
| Small effort | 1 |
| Worked at it | 11 |
| Worked hard | 24 |

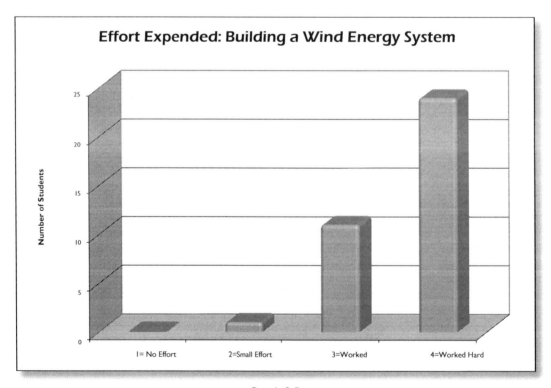

Graph 3.5

Students were also asked how successful they felt they were in this course, so far. The table and Graph 3.6 below show the indirect evidence collected based on their responses.

| Question 3: How Successful in Course? | |
|---|---|
| Very successful | 10 |
| Successful | 22 |
| Not successful | 4 |
| Missed it | 0 |

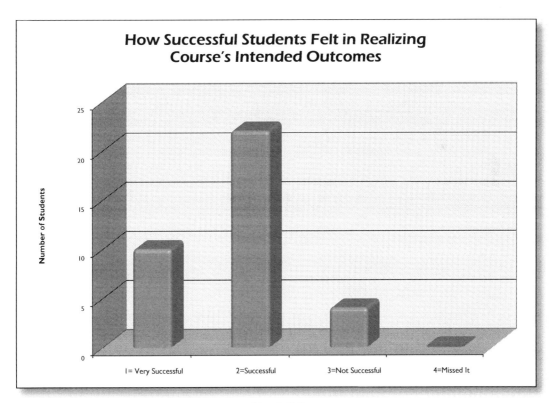

Graph 3.6

The AEP faculty also created a custom *Student Assessment of Instructor's Performance Checklist* (page 129), which asked students to assess the instructor using the ten Watermarks as criteria. The faculty used it in each of the AEP courses, in addition to a more generalized college and university faculty assessment form they felt was too limited. The real key to using indirect assessment tools of any sort is whether or not they generate meaningful and useful data.

# Template: Student Assessment of Instructor's Performance

**Purpose:** This assessment tool is based on the Ten Watermarks of Sound Instructional Practice, adopted by the Alternative Energy Technology faculty. It provides an opportunity for instructors to get an insight into how students like yourself believe the instructor demonstrated each practice.

Course #:_____    Instructor: _____    Date: _____

| Using the scale below, rate your instructor and place rating on line preceding each item below. | | | | |
| --- | --- | --- | --- | --- |
| 1 | 2 | 3 | 4 | 5 |
| Never | Seldom | Some of the time | Very often | Always |

**Question:** To what extent do you think your instructor demonstrated the following instructional practices?

_____  1.  From the very beginning of the course, made us aware of what we should be able to do in real-life roles as a result of what we were to learn in the course.

_____  2.  Created relevant tasks that challenged us and kept us engaged.

_____  3.  Made course content relevant to the intended real-life outcomes.

_____  4.  Gave us a clear picture of the whole course—how everything connected to the intended outcome.

_____  5.  Used strategies that encouraged interaction and collaborative learning.

_____  6.  Engaged with us in meaningful ways throughout the course.

_____  7.  Monitored our progress toward the intended outcomes and provided useful feedback.

_____  8.  Provided us with the standards and criteria for our work before we did the work.

_____  9.  Systematically gathered evidence of our successes and failures.

_____  10. Openly solicited and accepted feedback on how the learning experiences could be improved.

Total Score _____

Watermarks

The results of the *Student Assessment of Instructor* data for AEP 212 is shown in the chart below. According to these students, this data and graph show what Watermarks the AEP instructor modeled and which Watermarks they think could be improved upon. This information is important feedback for the classroom guide in making any future course adjustments and changes, as explained in the next section, ***Course Adjustment Planning Tool.***

## Average Assessment Ratings of Instructor per Watermark

3=Some of the time

4=Very often

5=Always

| Watermark # | Rating (1–5) |
| --- | --- |
| 1 | 4.50 |
| 2 | 4.10 |
| 3 | 3.20 |
| 4 | 4.60 |
| 5 | 4.95 |
| 6 | 3.50 |
| 7 | 4.60 |
| 8 | 4.30 |
| 9 | 4.00 |
| 10 | 4.20 |

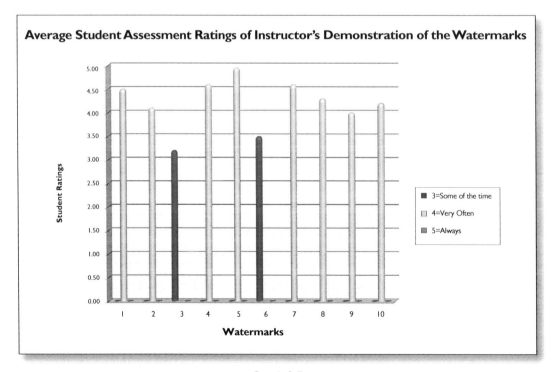

Graph 3.7

The students' assessment revealed that the majority of the Watermarks were well modeled by their AEP instructor. Nevertheless, two of the Watermarks were seen as being practiced some of the time. Is there a connection between their assessment here and Graphs 3.3 and 3.4 earlier, showing the students difficulties in analyzing their data?

In summary, the above seven data displays, including both direct and indirect learning evidence, became very useful when the AEP faculty approached Watermark X, *Adjust Practices Based on Evidence.*

## Template: Instructor's Self-Reflection and Assessment Checklist

**Purpose:** This assessment tool is based on the Ten Watermarks of Sound Instructional Practice. It provides an opportunity for you as an instructor to assess your application of these ten Watermarks.

Course #:_____    Instructor: _____    Date: _____

| | | | | |
|---|---|---|---|---|
| 1 | 2 | 3 | 4 | 5 |
| Never | Little | Sometimes | Very often | Always |

Using the scale below, rate your performance and place rating on line preceding each item below.

**Question:** To what extent do you think you demonstrated the following instructional practices?

_____ 1. **ENVISION REAL-LIFE OUTCOMES:** From the very beginning of the course, made students aware of what they should be able to do in real-life roles as a result of what they were to learn in the course; linked everything to the intended outcomes.

_____ 2. **CREATE ENERGY-GENERATING CHALLENGES:** Created relevant tasks that were increasingly difficult; challenged students and kept them engaged.

_____ 3. **ANALYZE OUTCOMES FOR ESSENTIAL CONTENT:** Made the course content relevant to the intended real-life outcomes.

_____ 4. **MAP THE JOURNEY:** Gave students a clear picture of the whole course—how everything connected to the intended outcome; kept them aware throughout the course.

_____ 5. **BUILD COMMUNITY:** Used strategies that encouraged interaction and collaborative learning.

_____ 6. **ENGAGE WITH LEARNERS TO BUILD PROFICIENCY:** Engaged with students in meaningful ways throughout the course.

_____ 7. **ASSESS TO ASSIST:** Monitored student progress toward the intended outcomes and provided useful feedback.

_____ 8. **ASSESS TO ADVANCE:** Provided students with the standards and criteria for their work before they did the work.

_____ 9. **GATHER AND TRACK LEARNING EVIDENCE:** Systematically gathered evidence of student successes and failures.

_____ 10. **ADJUST PRACTICES BASED ON EVIDENCE:** Openly solicited and accepted feedback on how to improve the learning experience.

Total Score _____

# COURSE ADJUSTMENT PLANNING TOOL

While most seasoned college instructors are accustomed to required program reviews every 3–5 years, under new accreditation standards, the review of learning evidence is an on-going, natural part of the guide's role. Course review at the end of a term or semester has been quite informal, if at all. The next few pages will illustrate how the AEP faculty formalized the process for all of their courses, which made the periodic program review much easier.

With a new commitment to improving the quality of every course, the AEP faculty decided to complete and share their course adjustment plans with each other at the end of each semester. They revised the *Student Assessment of Instructor Performance Tool*, page 129, into a self-assessment tool for AEP instructors (facing page), using the same standards (Watermarks) to which the students also responded. The comparison made very interesting and useful data.

After completing the above *Instructor's Self-Reflection and Assessment Checklist*, the AEP faculty compared their own ratings with those of the students. Here are the results of the AEP 212 instructor compared to the assessments by the students:

There was overall agreement across all Watermarks except for two. Students gave

| Application of Watermarks from Two Perspectives | | |
|---|---|---|
| Watermarks | Students' Average Rating per Watermark | Individual Instructor's Rating per Watermark |
| I | 4.50 | 4 |
| II | 4.10 | 5 |
| III | 3.20 | 4 |
| IV | 4.60 | 5 |
| V | 4.95 | 5 |
| VI | 3.50 | 5 |
| VII | 4.60 | 5 |
| VIII | 4.30 | 5 |
| IX | 4.00 | 4 |
| X | 4.20 | 4 |

lower average scores for Watermarks III and VI, respectively, compared to the classroom guide who rated application of the Watermarks much higher. This information was in addition to the learning evidence gathered earlier in the *Evidence Display Tools*.

The next step for the AEP classroom guide was to use the *Course Adjustment Planning Tool* to document changes to be made when AEP 212 is taught again. Figures 3.11a–c show the *Course Adjustment Planning Tool* as completed for AEP 212, including data graphs 3.1–3.7. A course adjustment template is provided on page 142 for your use.

## Course Adjustment Planning Tool (CAPT)

Course Title/#: <u>AEP 212: Alternative Energy Systems</u>  Term: <u>Fall 2011</u>
Instructor: <u>Greg Gunderson</u>  Program: <u>Alternative Energy Technology</u>

| Quality Indicators | Action Plan for Making Course Changes and Adjustments |
|---|---|
| A. Using the "Student Assessment of Instructor's Performance" and "Instructor's Self-Reflection and Assessment" checklists, examine your performance of the ten Watermarks. List or note any thoughts and key changes you plan to make in your future classroom guiding practices. Write the changes you want to make in the column to the right. | **Safety Glasses**: (Watermark III) Review safety procedure and especially the wearing of safety glasses during labs and other work sessions. Students seemed to disregard the concern for safety as an important issue. This may be related to Watermark III and my need to place more emphasis on this area of essential content.<br><br>**COG and MAP:** (Watermarks I, II, III, and IV) Use these two tools more often and review them consistently, even though at times I feel it is a waste of their time, but students say it is not. Students consistently asked for timelines related to tasks and assignments.<br><br>**Comments/Notes:** In addition to the two items above that I am aware of for adjustments in my teaching, students' assessments rated Watermarks III (essential content) and VI (build proficiency) lower than I did. I will analyze this further in Section B below. |

Figure 3.11a

| Quality Indicators | Action Plan for Making Course Changes and Adjustments |
|---|---|
| B. Attach and analyze any evidence displays (tables and graphs) of direct learning evidence (from authentic tasks such as key assessments, capstones, exams, tests) developed from Watermark IX, that suggests causes for course changes and/or adjustments. | **Data Analysis** (Watermark VI) Total student scores and overall scores for the three assessments show adequate academic performance (as shown in Graphs 3.1 and 3.2). A closer analysis of the three key assessments, *Quality Factor D: Data Analysis* (as shown in Graphs 3.3 and 3.4, show students having trouble explaining the variables and their interacting relationships (quality indicators 23–25). I need to add more time in class helping them to analyze these variables to build their learning proficiency. <br><br> **Graphing Techniques** (Watermarks III and VI) Students often presented graphs inaccurately and inappropriately (Graph 3.4, Questions 20–22). I will add more time explaining graphing techniques. <br><br> **Comments/Notes:** Learning Outcomes (Watermark I) are being achieved (Graph 3.1). Key Assessments (Watermark II), as noted in scoring guides and the capstone rubric, indicate they are relevant and challenging (Graph 3.2 below). No adjustments needed. |

Figure 3.11b

| Quality Indicators | Action Plan for Making Course Changes and Adjustments |
|---|---|
| C. Attach and analyze any data displays (tables and graphs) of indirect learning evidence (student observations, informal surveys) developed from Watermark IX that suggests causes for course changes and/or adjustments. | **Students Worked Hard:** (Watermarks I, V, VI) As indirect evidence (Graph 3.5 below), students reported to me that they worked hard and that the effort was worth the learning they received in return. This confirmed my feeling that I provided them with "good" classroom guiding—seems no changes are needed here. **Outcomes** (Watermark I) Students reported their satisfaction in meeting the course's intended outcomes (Graph 3.6). **Essential Content** (Watermark III) and **Build Proficiency** (Watermark VI) show a difference in perception as to how I carried out the Watermarks. These two Watermarks reveal a recurring pattern of difference between my students' assessments and my personal assessment (shown in the table below and in Graph 3.7). **Comments/Notes:** All learning evidence points to a need to make adjustments in how I present and review the essential content and in building the students' proficiency (Watermarks III and VI respectively in the table and Graph 3.7 on page 141). |

Figure 3.11c

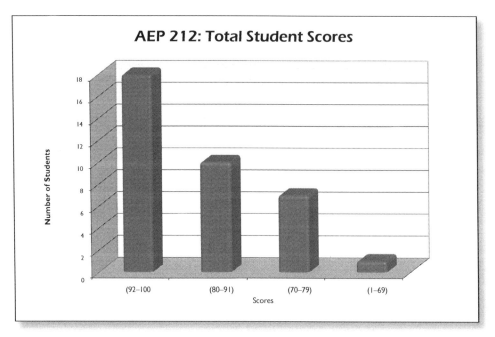

Graph 3.1

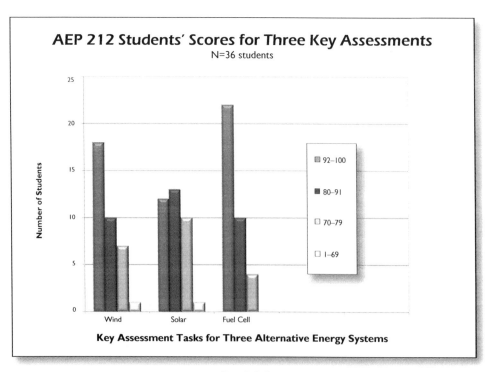

Graph 3.2

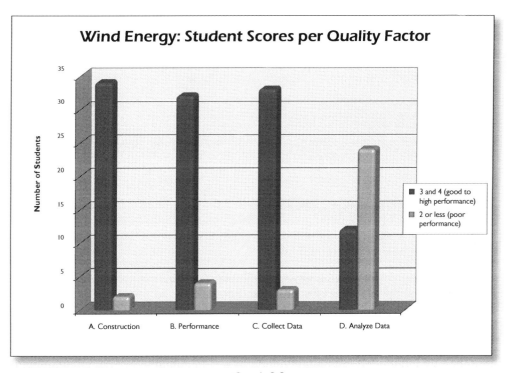

Graph 3.3

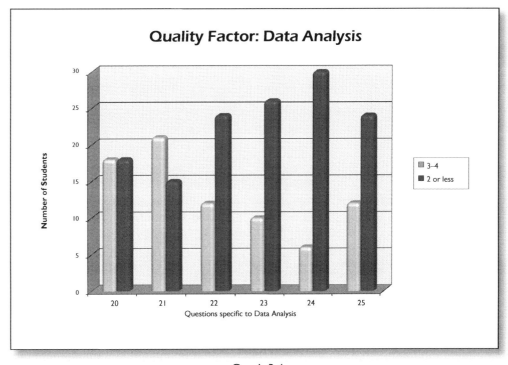

Graph 3.4

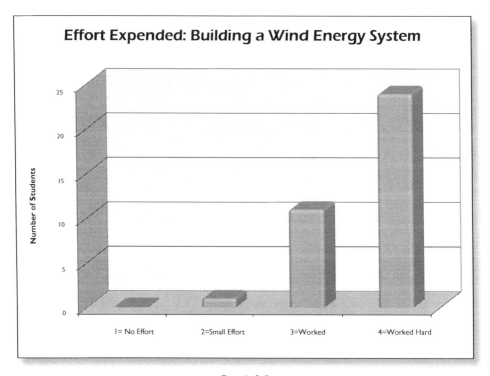

Graph 3.5

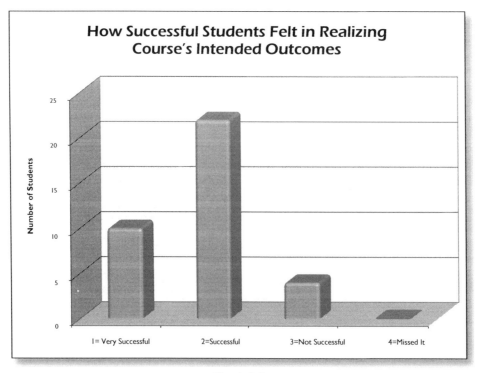

Graph 3.6

| Application of Watermarks from Two Perspectives | | |
| --- | --- | --- |
| Watermarks | Students' Average Rating per Watermark | Individual Instructor's Rating per Watermark |
| 1 | 4.50 | 4 |
| 2 | 4.10 | 5 |
| 3 | 3.20 | 4 |
| 4 | 4.60 | 5 |
| 5 | 4.95 | 5 |
| 6 | 3.50 | 5 |
| 7 | 4.60 | 5 |
| 8 | 4.30 | 5 |
| 9 | 4.00 | 4 |
| 10 | 4.20 | 4 |

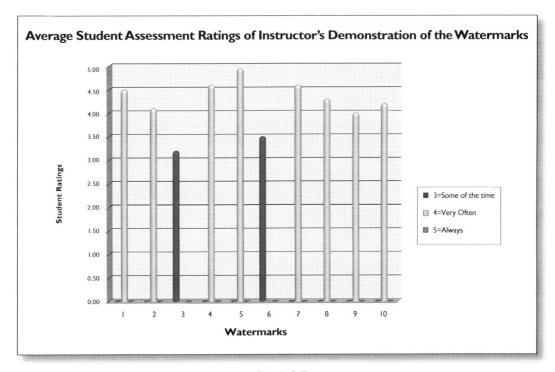

Graph 3.7

## Template: Course Adjustment Planning Tool (CAPT)

**Course Title:** _____  **Term:** _____

**Instructor:** _____  **Program:** _____

| Quality Indicators | Action Plan for Making Course Changes and Adjustments |
|---|---|
| A. Using the "Student Assessment of Instructor's Performance" and "Instructor's Self-Reflection and Assessment" checklists, examine your performance of the ten Watermarks. List or note any thoughts and key changes you plan to make in your future classroom guiding practices. Write the changes you want to make in the column to the right. | **Comments/Notes:** |
| B. Attach and analyze any evidence displays (tables and graphs) of direct learning evidence (from authentic tasks such as key assessments, capstones, exams, tests) developed from Watermark IX that suggests causes for course changes and/or adjustments. | **Comments/Notes:** |
| C. Attach and analyze any data displays (tables and graphs) of indirect learning evidence (student observations, informal surveys) developed from Watermark IX that suggests causes for course changes and/or adjustments. | **Comments/Notes:** |

# PART FOUR

# Supplemental Materials for Faculty Development Programs

We didn't want to finish this book without providing a few materials and suggestions for faculty development coordinators who might choose to use this book to focus their work with new, part-time, and adjunct instructors. Because this book is written specifically for course instructors, this section is brief.

## Three Major Suggestions

1. **Model the model.** Guiding faculty to better instructional performance is no different than what you expect them to do in guiding students. Modeling is your best strategy. Teach the Watermarks by modeling them in everything you do in your teaching improvement program. Don't just put together faculty workshops at random. Be strategic if you really want results.

    - Define your outcomes. (WM I)
    - Create specific challenges for them to demonstrate. (WM II)
    - Define the concepts, skills and issues that are central to achieving the level of proficiency you envision for the instructors. Don't pad it with irrelevant material. (WM III)
    - Map the process; share the map. (WM IV)
    - Build a community of learners. (WM V)
    - Engage with them in their learning. (WM VI)
    - Assess to assist them. (WM VII)
    - Assess to advance them. Make the achievement meaningful through certificates or recognitions by the college. (WM VIII)
    - Gather and track evidence of their progress. (WM IX)
    - Continually adjust your program based on the evidence of their progress. (WM X)

2.  **Use the unique power of the story and metaphor.** The story and river metaphor can be a common point of reference, regardless of the subject area. Use it to focus discussions; use it to emphasize the unpredictability of the journey and the power of an intended outcome.

3.  **Use our other resources.** We have three other books, written specifically for curriculum developers, that delve deeper into our work on learning outcomes and assessment. These books are listed under **Section V: *Recommended Readings*** and can only be purchased through The Learning Organization web site at *www.outcomesnet.com.*

To help you follow through on these suggestions, we have included these additional materials:

1.  Learning outcome statements for a faculty development program that reflect the Ten Watermarks of Sound Instructional Practice (page 147)

2.  A basic visual model that captures the characteristics of sound instructional practices (page 148)

3.  A glossary of river terms that will help you talk the metaphoric language of the river (page 149–52)

4.  A one-page synopsis of how the concepts of instructor as "guide" differs from the traditional concepts of college instructor (professor) as "teacher" (page 153)

The materials contained in Part Four of this book may be copied for use by faculty development programs in any college, provided credit is given to the authors. All other parts of the book (except for blank tools and checklists) are protected under copyright and may not be reproduced in any form.

# Ten Strategic Outcomes for Improvement of Teaching Programs in Colleges and Universities

College and university programs for improving teaching and learning should be guided by a clear set of learning outcomes in the same fashion as academic courses, and should model the desired characteristics of sound instructional practice. Below are the outcome statements based on the model presented in this book.

*Faculty should be able to:*

**Envision real-life outcomes**
Work collaboratively to envision and articulate intended learning outcomes in context of life roles; focus on the intended outcomes in designing the course/program.

**Create energy-generating challenges**
Create engaging tasks that challenge the students to do something relevant to their lives and provide opportunity for assessment of intended outcomes.

**Analyze outcomes for essential content**
Analyze intended outcomes to determine what students need to learn.

**Map the journey**
Provide a map that informs students where they are going and where they are in relation to the intended outcomes.

**Build community**
Build a learning environment and a sense of community among learners.

**Engage with learners to build proficiency**
Directly engage with learners to build proficiency, increase retention and increase student success.

**Assess to assist**
Monitor and provide on-going feedback using defined criteria.

**Assess to advance**
Advance learners based on evidence of achieved intended learning outcomes;

**Gather and track learning evidence**
Gather and track both direct and indirect evidence of learning.

**Adjust practice based on evidence**
Use learning evidence to make on-going adjustments in student learning experiences.

# Ten Watermarks

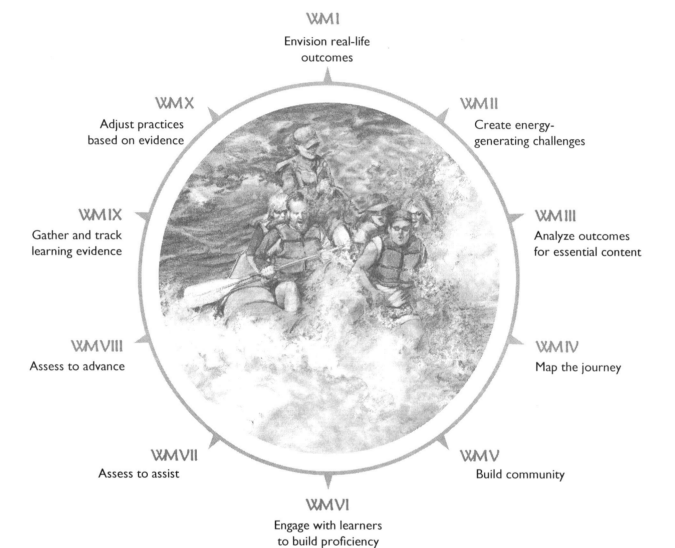

**WM I**
Envision real-life outcomes

**WM X**
Adjust practices based on evidence

**WM II**
Create energy-generating challenges

**WM IX**
Gather and track learning evidence

**WM III**
Analyze outcomes for essential content

**WM VIII**
Assess to advance

**WM IV**
Map the journey

**WM VII**
Assess to assist

**WM V**
Build community

**WM VI**
Engage with learners to build proficiency

## of Sound Instructional Practice

## Glossary of River Terms Applied to College Learning Experiences

## *Words that describe THE RIVER:*

**RIVER**

A natural body of flowing water of considerable volume, constant and always changing.

*A body of knowledge, constant and always changing, structured as curriculum and expressed as concepts, skills, and issues a student must navigate to reach the intended outcomes.*

**WATER**

The liquid that descends from clouds and forms streams, lakes, and seas.

*Concepts, issues, and skills that descend from a knowledge base to form a curriculum*

**WHITEWATER RAPIDS**

A highly dynamic system of predictable and unpredictable water formed when a river's gradient increases enough to disturb its flow and create turbulence resulting in a rapid.

*A challenging course where the level of difficulty increases and turbulence is experienced.*

**CONFLUENCE**

A flowing together of two streams, integrated into something bigger and fuller, larger than the sum of the parts

*Synthesis of learning; high order thinking of analysis and synthesis.*

**DESTINATION**

An intended take-out point; the end of a section of the river.

*Intended student learning outcomes to be achieved at the end of a course or academic program.*

# Words that describe CHALLENGES OF THE RIVER:

**FLAT WATER**
Presents the unique challenge of continuing to paddle a fully loaded raft for miles with no energy from the river.

*Deep content, requiring persistence and tenacity*

**CLASS LEVELS**
A label and rating system designating the level of difficulty of a rapid, from easy (I) to unrunnable (VI).

*Level of learning difficulty in a course.*

**WAKE-UP RAPID**
Whitewater that follows flat water and comes on rather abruptly

*A challenging work task or test that follows newly-learned material; often a non-graded surprise quiz or task to determine learners' degree of understanding of content*

**WATER RESCUE**
Presents the unique challenge for both guide and paddlers in rescuing a paddler who falls from the raft.

*When one or more students experiencing learning difficulty is assisted by others.*

**BOULDER GARDEN**
Obstacles in the river seemingly strewn everywhere

*What it looks like when learning gets tough.*

**STRAINER**
An obstruction (e.g tree limb) in the river that allows water to pass through and around but will ensnare a person or a raft.

*Serious obstructions or challenges to learning.*

**SLEEPER**
An obstruction in the river that lies just below the water's surface on which a raft can lodge.

*An invisible obstruction to learning.*

| **MAYTAG HOLE** | A spot in the river that takes on the characteristic of a washing machine; also known as a suck hole, pulling rafts into its circular motion. |

*A concept or skill that a student can't seem to "get."*

## Words that describe RIVER RAFTERS/RUNNERS:

**PADDLERS**

Persons who have few, some, or many skills to navigate the river with the help of a guide.

*Students*

**RIVER GUIDE**

A skilled person who understands and knows a whitewater river and who, through the use of a paddle oar and specific commands to paddlers, controls the direction of the raft down the river.

*Class instructor—guide*

**TEAMWORK**

The essential collaboration of both guide and paddlers working together to get them both successfully down a river

*A collaborative way to achieve learning outcomes.*
*A learning community which collectively knows who they are, where they are, and where they are going.*

## Words that describe RUNNING THE RIVER:

**PADDLE RAFTS**

16-to-20-foot inflated rubber boat that must be paddled by all aboard, in contrast to an oar raft in which the guide does all the work.

*Learning experiences that engage the students and the instructor.*

**PUT-IN**

The location where rafters enter a section of the river.

*The first meeting or session of a new class or course.*

**PUT-IN TALK**

A river guide's talk on what paddlers need to do to ensure a successful trip down the river.

*A classroom guide's talk on what students need to know and do to be successful in a class or course.*

**TAKE-OUT**

The location on a river where the trip ends and when both river guides and rafters pull the raft from the water.

*The last meeting or session of a class or course, when both classroom guide and students reflect on successes and steps for continued improvement.*

**SCOUTING STOP**

An intentional stop to observe the entire rapid ahead and assess the skills of the paddlers against the upcoming challenge.

*An intentional stop in a class or course to observe the entire journey and assess where learners are.*

**EDDYING OUT**

Pulling into quiet water along the shore to take a break.

*Taking a purposeful pause to reflect on one's learning.*

**MANEUVERABILITY**

Ability to adjust to changing conditions using a set of paddling strokes that strategically move the raft through sections and rapids of the river.

*Ability to adjust to changing directions and conditions for learning.*

**RIDE THE BULL**

A paddler, sitting on the front edge of the raft, challenges self to ride through a rapid.

*A learner taking on a new risk or challenge in a class or course.*

## Comparing Practices Across Two Teaching Frameworks

| College Instructor as "GUIDE" | College Instructor as "Professor/Lecturer" |
| --- | --- |
| **Focus**<br>Building student proficiency in real-life outcomes | **Focus**<br>Covering content |
| **Destination**<br>Learning is a process which should result in clearly intended outcomes. | **Destination**<br>Getting through the textbook |
| **Engagement (practice)**<br>Students and guide are engaged together as a learning community to achieve the learning outcomes; practice of newly-learned content is structured into class time. | **Engagement (practice)**<br>Mostly from the "stage;" lecturing is the preferred mode, and there is no time for practice in class. |
| **Responsibility/Accountability**<br>Students and guide share responsibility for the learning outcomes | **Responsibility/Accountability**<br>Students are responsible for their own learning. |
| **Relevance**<br>Higher learning is connected to real-life roles in the community, workplace, family, and global society. | **Relevance**<br>Depth of knowledge is more desired than application. |
| **Standards**<br>Criteria for student performance is public knowledge. | **Standards**<br>Tests should be hidden from students. |
| **Assessment**<br>Assessment is a learning motivator, not a penalty, and focuses on simulated work performance. | **Assessment**<br>Assessment means testing, and testing separates "the men from the boys." |

## Resources and Contacts

For additional support and assistance in using this work, go to the White Water Institute web site at *www.white-waterinstitute.com* for:

1. Free, digitized files for all templates included in Part Three of this book,

2. Updated schedules for actual river experiences and professonal development with the White Water Institute for Instructional Leadership, and

3. Contact with the authors.

PART FIVE

# Recommended Readings

*T*his book, written specifically for instructors, is the finishing piece of the *Outcomes Primer Series* developed by The Learning Organization to assist colleges in reconstructing their curriculum to meet emerging accreditation standards for learning outcomes assessment.

## The Outcomes Primer Series

The in-depth series is available only through The Learning Organization at *www.outcomesnet.com*.

Stiehl, Ruth and Lewchuk, Les (2008). *The Outcomes Primer: Reconstructing the College Curriculum* (3rd ed.). Corvallis, Oregon: The Learning Organization.
ISBN 978-9637457-4-3

Stiehl, Ruth and Lewchuk, Les (2012). *The MAPPING Primer: Tools for Reconstructing the College Curriculum* (2nd ed.). Corvallis, Oregon: The Learning Organization.
ISBN: 0-9637457-3-5

Stiehl, Ruth and Lewchuk, Les (2008). *The ASSESSMENT Primer: Creating a Flow of Evidence*. Corvallis, Oregon: The Learning Organization.
ISBN: 978-9637457-5-0

A bibliography of the interdisciplinary research and literature that supports this body of work can be found in each of the three books listed above under the following general areas:

Visual Design

Systems Thinking—ecology

Systems Thinking—organization and development

Systems Thinking—visual tools

College Curriculum Development

Discipline Integration

Studies associated with this work

# About the Authors

### Don Prickel, Ph.D.

EDUCATIONAL CONSULTANT

PAST PRESIDENT, WHITE WATER INSTITUTE FOR COLLEGE

INSTRUCTIONAL LEADERSHIP, ASTORIA, OREGON

Dr. Prickel is both a national and international educational consultant in outcomes-based curriculum design and adult learner-centered instructional practices for community colleges and universities. He is co-author of *Number Power: Geometry and Number Power: Graphs, Charts, Schedules, and Maps*, Contemporary Books/McGraw Hill, Inc. His experiences as an adult educator, teacher trainer, assistant professor and coordinator of a master's degree program in adult education at Oregon State University have resulted in this unique resource for adult college faculty.

In partnership with Dr. Stiehl, Dr. Prickel continues to work closely with colleges to transform traditional teaching practices into guiding adult learners through engaged and innovative practices. Formerly President of the Board of Directors of the White Water Institute, he resides in both Corvallis, Oregon and Tucson, Arizona.

*www.white-waterinstitute.com*

### Dr. Ruth E. Stiehl, Ed.D.

PROFESSOR EMERITUS,

INSTRUCTIONAL LEADERSHIP IN HIGHER EDUCATION,

OREGON STATE UNIVERSITY

Dr. Stiehl is best known as co-author of a series of three books on learning outcomes and assessment: *The Outcomes Primer: Reconstructing the College Curriculum*, 2nd Ed. (2007), *The Assessment Primer: Creating a Flow of Evidence* (2009), and *The Mapping Primer: Tools for Reconstructing the College Curriculum*, 2nd Ed. (2012). Over a period of ten years, this series has helped hundreds of colleges across the United States and Canada to meet new accreditation standards for learning and assessment that is more relevant to life roles in the 21st century.

In contrast to most scholarly and academic works, all of Dr. Stiehl's teaching, writing, speaking, and workshops are charged with story, metaphor, and experiential engagement. A cofounder of the White Water Institute, she lives and works in Corvallis, Oregon.

*www.outcomesnet.com*
*www.white-waterinstitute.com*

Made in the USA
Charleston, SC
29 March 2012